THE CROSSROADS OF CHAMPIONS

MANHOOD, MILITARY, MARRIAGE, AND MINISTRY:

The Interconnectedness of
the lives of Rev. Dr. Johnny Clarence Bachus
and Marvin Mims Sr.

MARVIN MIMS SR.

Copyright 2022 © Marvin Mims Sr. All rights reserved.

No part of this publication may be reproduced, distributed or transmitted in any form or by any means, including photocopying, recording or other electronic or mechanical methods, without the prior written permission of the publisher, except in case of brief quotations embodied in reviews and other non-commercial uses permitted by copyright law. Permission requests can be emailed to the publisher as listed below.

Published in the United States by Marvin Mims Sr.
Memphis, TN
boldtn04@yahoo.com

Edited by Lynn E. Ballard
lynnconnects@gmail.com

Names: Mims, Marvin Sr., Author | Ballard, Lynn E., Editor
Title: The Crossroads of Champions: Manhood, Marriage, Military and Ministry. The Interconnectedness of the lives of Rev. Dr. Johnny Clarence Bachus and Marvin Mims Sr. | Marvin Mims, Sr.
Description: Memphis, TN, self-published by Marvin Mims Sr.
Subjects: Autobiography – United States | | African American Families – United States | Black Church – United States | Black Baptists Preachers – United States | Memphis, TN – United States | Mental Health – United States | Ministry – United States | Pastorship – United States | Racism in the Military – United States |

ISBN: 979-8-218-06194-4

Cover Design by M.G. Ballard Designs, mg@mgballarddesigns.com

DEDICATION

To the memory of my late parents

ANDREW WILLIE MIMS SR. and TEREATHER ADDIE "PEACHES" RUSSELL MIMS

whose love and guidance nurtured me on the path to a blessed life

To my beloved grandsons

HAZEN DESMOND WALKER and ADDISON JOSHUA "HAPPY" WALKER

who fill my heart and soul with immeasurable pride and joy

TABLE OF CONTENTS

Foreword 1

Preface 3

Chapter One: The Road to Manhood & Memphis 7

Chapter Two: The Military, Marriage & Back to Memphis 35

Chapter Three: Maneuvering Military Roads 69

Chapter Four: Marriage, Family & Mental Health
"The Man in the Mirror" 97

Chapter Five: Ministry Crossroads 121

Chapter Six: Rev. Dr. Johnny Clarence ("J.C.") Bachus "Cowboy" 157

Chapter Seven: The Crossroads of Champions 191

Chapter Eight: Pastor, Priest & Prophet 211

Tributes to Rev. Dr. Johnny Clarence ("J.C.") Bachus 241

Acknowledgments 251

FOREWORD

My name is Archie L. Thomas, and I serve as Senior Pastor of Living Word Cathedral Church of God in Christ in Osceola, Arkansas. It has been my pleasure to know Marvin Mims Sr. since 1991 and to serve as a spiritual brother and advisor to him for many years. Our relationship started as co-workers, we soon became neighbors, and we grew into best friends and fellow ministers of the gospel of Christ. Our brotherly connection is truly divine, and our families share a close bond like blood relatives.

Over the years, I have witnessed Marvin's unwavering love and devotion to his precious wife Anita, his accomplished children and grandchildren, and his spiritual father, the late Rev. Dr. Johnny C. Bachus. *The Crossroads of Champions* is a masterpiece about his life and Rev. Dr. Bachus' and how the lives of these two men from Mississippi intersected at various crossroads. They encouraged and supported each other in family life and ministry, through trials and triumphs, for forty years. Mims gives us insight into his struggles and triumphs as a Black man in the U.S. military and the spiritual guidance he received from one of the greatest preachers of our times. When you read about their journeys and how they overcame obstacles, you will learn something about being a champion, hopefully in a way that inspires your life!

Marvin exemplifies the traits of a servant leader: humility, altruism, vision, and trust. My brother's steadfast devotion to God, leadership & family has been a prototype of faith in the Lord. I am thankful for my friend, his love, his giving spirit, his heart of caring, and the words of hope he has given to the world.

Thanking God for you,

Superintendent Archie L. Thomas Jr., Senior Pastor

Living Word Cathedral Church of God in Christ

PREFACE

I have a two-fold purpose for writing this book. First, to share my life story as a Black man living in America. Too often, the narrative on Black men is one-dimensional. Framing Black men in a way that makes us seem *less than* diminishes our spirit, manhood, and humanity. My journey highlights the challenges of manhood, ministry, marriage, and the military but also my triumphs. I hope my story resonates with readers, particularly young Black men. I hope they see a champion in themselves.

The second purpose is to document the life of the late Rev. Dr. Johnny C. Bachus. My life was changed forever in 1979 when our crossroads began. To say he was a champion is an understatement. As his son-in-law, I observed the Lord anointing him to equip people to grow in Christ and expand the Kingdom of God for more than four decades. I witnessed him operate in all dimensions of the five-fold ministry: apostle, prophet, evangelist, pastor, and teacher. EPHESIANS 4:11 I saw his ministry rise to great heights and slowly regress in later years. His faith never wavered.

This book started with me writing his biography, a project I began in December 2014. That was the year he was honored by the National Baptist Convention, USA, for fifty years of continuous service as pastor of St. Mark Missionary Baptist Church in Memphis, Tennessee. His rich legacy of service was a motivating factor in documenting his life and ministry.

I was excited to have Pastor Bachus' blessing on this project. Unfortunately, it veered off course when other life demands got in my way. By 2020, the Coronavirus pandemic was forcing people around the globe to slow down, shut in, and distance themselves from regular routines. That extra time gave me a chance to get back on track with writing Pastor Bachus' biography and time to think about my journey. Around this time, I felt inspired to also write about my life. I had a hard time deciding which path to focus on, mine or Pastor Bachus'. After consulting with two close friends and spiritual advisors, Pastor Ronald Hampton and Pastor Archie Thomas, I combined the work into one book that tells our stories and highlights our crossroads.

Often what some people view as a blessed life is accompanied by adversity, depression, opposition, and overcoming personal challenges and conflict within the home and on the job. In *Chapter Four: Marriage, Family & Mental Health,* I discuss the mental health counseling that helped me confront the man in the mirror.

Pastor Bachus was humbled by the thought of me creating a

historical account of his life and ministry. That was characteristic of his personality. We met privately numerous times in his pastor's study at St. Mark to recount defining moments in his life and ministry. At other times, we had conversations at his home, surrounded by family. In *Chapter Eight: Pastor, Priest, and Prophet,* I share some of the ingredients he poured into me on how to be a successful pastor and lead God's flock. Completing this book became an even greater priority when his health began to decline. I regret not finishing it before he passed in April 2021, but I am confident he knew how important it was to me to memorialize his legacy.

A crossroad is many things - a point at which an important choice has to be made, a place where two roads meet, a time when lives intersect. I hope the way our lives intersected will be an inspiration to you.

Lastly, neither Pastor Bachus nor I can stake a claim to wealth, fame, or anything like that when it comes to being a champion. We don't have gold rings to showcase victories, and you won't find our names engraved on a wall of heroes. Still, we are champions.

We are champions because we are sons of the Mississippi Delta who thrived in our childhoods there despite its history of racism and poverty. The love we received from family, church, and community guided both of us on the path to manhood.

We are champions because we arrived in Memphis with only family to lean on, loved ones who didn't have much more than open arms to help us get on our feet. We never took their generosity for granted or gave up on ourselves. We took bold steps in pursuit of our dreams.

We are champions because we've loved and cared for our wives, children, grandchildren, and others.

We are champions because we sacrificed to protect and uplift our communities and this nation. We've taken stands against racism and oppression and been our brothers' keepers when it wasn't easy.

We are champions because we love the Lord and didn't resist when the Holy Spirit called us to preach. We are champions because we put our trust in the Lord and kept our faith.

We are champions because God loves us.

We are champions because we love you.

Marvin Mims, Sr.

August 2022

CHAPTER ONE

The Road to Manhood & Memphis

My family's roots in the Mississippi Delta go back several generations. When slavery ended, the Mississippi Delta experienced a migration of African Americans into the area in places that provided an opportunity to purchase land relatively cheaply. My maternal great-great-grandparents, Henry Richardson and Jane Ann Bernard Richardson, were part of that migration. They moved from Louisiana to Bolivar County, Mississippi, and settled in a small town named Shaw, where farming and growing cotton was the way of life.

Their daughter Adeline was born in 1872. Growing up, we were told she was "part Indian," as it was said back then. We don't know her exact Native American ancestry. It's a blessing I knew her and was able to spend time with her in Shaw. I was eight years old when she passed in 1968.

Adeline was married to a legendary figure in our family, my maternal great-grandfather, James Henry Russell Sr., who we lovingly called "Papa." When they married on September 22, 1894, both had a fourth-grade education, a significant achievement for those times since they could both read and write. They worked hard and, by 1920, owned their land "free and clear."[1]

Papa Russell was born in Philadelphia, Mississippi, which decades later became the site of one of the most well-known tragedies of the Civil Rights Movement, the 1964 murder of Civil Rights Workers James Chaney, Andrew Goodman, and Michael Schwerner. When Papa left Philadelphia, he spearheaded generations of entrepreneurship in our family. He purchased 80 acres of land in Shaw, built a general store for Adeline to operate next to their house, and developed an outstanding reputation for professional expertise in carpentry, bricklaying, masonry, and architecture. Some individuals in the community would only contract services with him. He was a visionary man whose multiple trades and skills provided him with several streams of income. Although his plans to purchase an additional 1,000 acres of land did not come to fruition, he gifted the generations behind him by passing on land and a spirit of self-determination.

When Papa died, he left the 80 acres of farmland in Shaw to his sons. Two of them, John T. Russell and James Henry Russell Jr., chose not to pursue farming and moved north to Gary, Indiana.

---

[1] 1920 United States Federal Census. James H. Russell. Mississippi, Sunflower, Beat 4, District 0121.

Another son, William Russell, pursued his passion in brick masonry, which left little time for him to assist with the farm. His youngest son, my grandfather Sandy Clifton Russell, Sr., became the property's principal farmer. Granddaddy Russell farmed and managed the land for many years, raising chickens and pigs, and growing cotton, corn, beans, vegetables, watermelons, and peanuts. He not only inherited his father's entrepreneurial spirit; he was also a true leader.

Granddaddy Russell and his wife Thelma raised their children in Shaw. My mother, Tereather "Peaches" Addie Russell Mims, was their third child. The family story is that she got her nickname "Peaches" because Grandmother Thelma ate so many of them while she was pregnant with her. Their four sons had a significant influence on my life: Sylvester (Uncle Little), Sandy Jr. (Uncle June), Robert Sr. (Uncle Robert), and especially James Henry (Uncle Jake). They also had another beautiful daughter her name was Eliza Mae Russell-Phillips.

My father, Andrew Willie Mims Sr., was also born and raised in Shaw. His mother wasn't married, and times were hard, so he was raised by his grandmother, Luella Dixon, who we called "Mommy Sissy." Like my maternal grandparents, my father's grandparents also worked on a farm growing cotton. His mother was Lueddie Love, who was lovingly called "Dude."

The Crossroads of Champions

My parents lived within a 5-mile radius of each other growing up, and both came from large families. As a kid, my father played with my mother's brothers until, according to her brother Sylvester, she came "up outta nowhere and took him!" My uncles maintained their close bonds with my dad throughout their lives. They saw him as a generous man who loaned them his car in times of need. Uncle Sylvester nicknamed him "Doug" and described him as being a *man* above *boys*. He and Mom told us the story about how Momma Sissy required my dad to pick 200 pounds of cotton a day, which was way above the norm. Instead, he'd pick above 200 pounds to sell the rest on the side for his profit.

My parents married in 1955, the "golden age" of marriage in the U.S. when marriage rates were high. They were relatively young when they married, my father was 19 years old, and my mother was only 16. Granddaddy Russell told my father, "If you don't want her, bring her back where you got her from."

It's no wonder the Mississippi Delta gave birth to the blues. The ebb and flow of rivers, cotton fields with laborers toiling under Mississippi's brutal sun, racism, economic hardship, and in the midst of it all, a natural yearning for love and something more. My parents worked on farms and in the cotton fields as teenagers. To escape that kind of hard manual labor, they married young and left Shaw for something better. My father enlisted in the United States Army ten days after they married. He served from 1958 to 1961 in Pittsburgh, Pennsylvania. My mother often spoke fondly of their time there, referring to it as a great experience.

After leaving Pennsylvania, they planted roots in the city of Greenville, Mississippi. The Greenville I was born and raised in is actually the third place in Mississippi with that name. Little remains of the first place, now known as "Old Greenville." In the early 1800s, it was an important center of plantations and cotton gins, but it declined rapidly when the county seat was moved from Greenville to Fayette in 1825. The second Greenville was destroyed during the Civil War. After angry locals shot at Union soldiers for docking a boat there, the soldiers retaliated by burning every building in town to the ground. The Greenville that survived all of that is where I grew up, a port city on the east bank of the Mississippi River, a part of the Mississippi Delta.

Cotton was still king in the Delta, but Greenville had a diverse economy that included other agricultural commodities, steel fabricators, and mercantile businesses. That diversity fueled population growth in the 1950s. By the time I was born in July 1960, Greenville had grown to a thriving city of over 40,000 people.

My only sister Angela ("Ann") was the firstborn. I was the second child and eldest of my parents' four sons. Following behind me in successive order are Andrew Willie Mims Jr., nicknamed "So"; Morris Donald Mims ("Don"); and my youngest brother Derek Russell Mims who called me his twin because we looked alike. As children, we all had different personalities. Ann was the boss! While I was always loud and outgoing, Andrew was quiet. Don was outspoken and had a smart mouth that led to his being slapped by our mother on a few occasions. Still, he clung to her and learned one of her greatest gifts and passions, cooking! Derek was full of joy and excitement. He was the baby boy and the only child Dad wouldn't allow Mom to discipline, probably because he was born so much later in their lives. He loved the church. A bible verse that was dear to him is ST. JOHN 10:11, *"I am the good shepherd: the good shepherd giveth his life for the sheep."* Derek often got into trouble, but he had a good heart, and our family and everyone in the community loved him. Health issues caused his early death.

My parents settled on Abraham Street after living on Joy Street and 6th Street. Abraham means "father of a multitude." Those two blocks proved to be a blessed street with twenty or more families when we were growing up. My father and mother were middle-class, hard-working people with decent incomes from their jobs with steel companies. We lived in a three-bedroom house with one bath, a kitchen, and a living room. My father made sure our family had nice automobiles, regularly investing in new cars and always keeping them clean. He also kept us clean! I distinctly recall him scrubbing dirt off my body after I played all day outdoors. When he finished scrubbing, I felt brand new, too!

Each night we sat at the table and ate dinner together as siblings. Our family kept a black and white television in the boys' bedroom. On Friday nights, the whole family enjoyed gathering there to watch sitcoms like *Sanford and Son, Flip Wilson,* and *The Jeffersons.* Each night around 10:30 p.m., the television signed off with the National Anthem, and then the screen went blank. If you wanted to watch something past then, you were out of luck. This was long before cable television made shows available twenty-four hours a day.

Mom was a woman of preparation. She ironed our clothes and placed them in a dresser drawer. The night before school, she laid our clothes for that day on top of her dresser. Greenville had one high school and three junior high schools. Racial divides were prevalent during that time, even affecting even us kids. I remember divisions between white and black students leading to fights in elementary school. Even so, I didn't have my first direct experience with racism until after I left Greenville. As a young child, I was too busy playing baseball and football to care about what white people thought about us. My biggest worry back then was my sister Ann who was the "mom" of the house when our real mother was at work.

When my parents left us at home, Ann was always in charge. Our constant struggles for power intensified as I got older. I felt being the firstborn son, I should have more power, but being the firstborn child, Ann refused to relinquish it. She would limit my coming in and out of the house during summer. I loved playing outdoors and always wanted cold water from the refrigerator. Ann placed the house on lockdown, forcing me to drink water from the outdoor faucet.

There was very little cooking done by us kids during the summer. We mostly ate canned food like potted meat, bologna sandwiches, or peanut butter and jelly sandwiches and drank a lot of milk. My brothers and I went through two gallons of milk every week, and Mom accused me of drinking milk for water because I loved it so much. When the milk ran out, we had to wait until she went to the grocery store on Fridays to buy some more.

It was a blessing to grow up during a time when neighbors cared about each other. One childhood memory of their caring has stuck with me all my life. When I was about ten years old, I was boiling an egg on the stove for my brother Don when somehow the pot of hot water spilled on my stomach and burned me badly. I was in excruciating pain when I ran to a friend's house nearby. His mother quickly placed butter on my stomach, a common home remedy for severe burns, and called Dad. He rushed home from work to take me to the hospital, and Mom left her job and met us there. I had second-degree burns on my stomach, resulting in severe pain and skin blisters. My parents weren't upset because we were allowed to cook on the stove. However, after this incident, Mom banned us from cooking on the stove. The psychological impact of this incident still lingers with me today. I never use the front burners on a stove and discourage Anita from using them, especially when our grandchildren visit us.

Our neighborhood wasn't perfect. We had a few bullies, but we played together in harmony for the most part. I developed close relationships with some of the kids I grew up with who were like brothers to me. I spent most of my time playing outdoors with my friends Dale Hodges, who we called "Blab," Ricky Taliaferro, Wanda Howard, Erica Draine and her brother Lloyd who we called "Tiger," Victoria James, and Burley Hopkins. My best friend growing up was also my neighbor and mentor, Terry Sibley. And what would a childhood be without a childhood sweetheart? Mine was Mary Ann James. Steve Sutton was a great friend at school.

I rarely played inside with my siblings. Andrew wasn't into sports or playing outdoors like me and was much more laid back than

I was. Don was much younger, and he bonded with friends his age. I was always organizing an activity in the community, usually a game of sports or something that brought people together in some other way, a skill I carried into the military and ministry. Of course, Ann was busy managing the house, so she didn't have time to play with us.

Our schools didn't offer many activities outside the campus, but in the sixth grade, I was able to travel to Memphis, Tennessee, for a school field trip and to visit the Memphis Zoo. Later as a teenager, Uncle Jake allowed me to travel to Kansas City, Kansas, to spend the summer with his family. Those were my two major trips growing up, and they allowed me to get a glimpse of life outside the Delta.

Our family travel was limited to visiting close family who lived near us. One of my childhood joys was making the 40-mile journey every two weeks to visit my grandparents and cousins in Shaw, Mississippi. Shaw was a very small town that only had gravel and dirt roads. There were no modern conveniences like we had in Greenville, and the grocery store was miles away. There were cotton fields everywhere. Shaw was "the country," and I loved visiting there.

I remember churning butter manually as a child and my grandmother and cousins washing clothes on a washboard and hanging them on a line. I loved it when Granddaddy Russell gave me rides on his tractor. I viewed Granddaddy Russell as poor because he was a farmer and a hard worker, and I didn't realize his greatness and entrepreneurship until I became an adult. He significantly impacted my life as I often witnessed his generosity towards others. Every time we visited, Granddaddy Russell gave us bags of frozen peas, beans, corn, sweet potatoes, and other food from his freezer. One memorable occurrence of his giving happened when Anita and I visited him early in our marriage. As we were leaving, he gave us a sweet potato pie that had already been cut. I looked at the table, saw a whole pie, and asked him for it. He graciously gave it to us.

Uncle Jake, Uncle Little, Uncle Robert, Uncle June, and their families visited us every summer and a couple of times throughout the year. Small spaces seem to expand in some way when welcoming family. I remember my parents generously giving up their bedroom to Uncle Little and his wife Katherine when they traveled from California each summer to spend a week with us. Uncle June lived in Fulton, Kentucky, and Uncle Robert lived in Kansas City, Kansas, along with Uncle Jake. These reunions kept our family ties strong.

Growing up, our grandparents always gave us quarters, which could buy a lot of candy back then. However, we hit the big times when Uncle Jake and Uncle Robert visited. They gave us dollar bills which made me feel like we were rich! That was big money!

Of all my uncles, I developed the closest relationship with Uncle Jake. He was so positive and uplifting in his disposition and our conversations. His constant encouragement made me feel special, like I could accomplish anything in life. It meant a lot that he treated me more like a son than a nephew.

Thinking back, our family has always been generous. Like her father and brothers, my mother was very giving. She was always baking cakes for people and giving them away. She made the best homemade pound cakes, chocolate cakes, and jelly cakes. She'd let me lick the bowl of cake mix, which was delicious! Mom gave her time to people in the community, picking them up for church and checking on people who were shut in.

My father was a quiet man who, in some ways, led by example. He worked two jobs for many years and taught me the value of hard work as a teenager. After teaching me how to operate a lawnmower, he made me responsible for mowing our lawn. Then he signed me up for a paper route with the *Delta Democrat-Times*, the local newspaper company. I rode my bike in the sunshine, rain, and extreme cold and heat to deliver papers on my route. On Sunday mornings, I had to get up at 3:30 a.m. so I could deliver the newspaper to over 100 customers and return home to prepare for Sunday school by 9:00 a.m. My dad would take me in his car if the weather was really bad, and he was good at throwing newspapers out of his Volkswagen window and driving at the same time.

After some persuading, a few of the customers on my newspaper route allowed me to cut their lawns during the summer months. I used my bike to pull our family lawnmower behind me for the few miles I traveled to cut yards. At other times I would canvas our neighborhood to see if anyone else wanted their yard cut. This proved to be profitable as well. During my childhood, I would make between $3 to $7 cutting a large front- and backyard, sometimes $10 if the customer was generous. The price for mowing a similar yard today is $35 to $85. By 13 years old, I was making good money delivering newspapers to residents. After I had been delivering newspapers for several years, the *Delta Democrat-Times* converted all their routes to service by adults. I continued working with an adult to deliver papers, but it became more of a business than an opportunity for youth to be employed independently.

I cannot recall a time as a young person when I did not have money. Most of it came honestly through hard work, but I lifted $20 bills a few times off my dad's dresser or out of his pants pocket. I believe I stole from him because he had so much money and never seemed to count it. I think our daughter Tracy got me back for those times, but I don't have any proof.

When I was 16 years old, I spent the summer with my father's mother, who we called "Madea," a cross between "Mother" and "Dearest," and a southern term for grandmother. Madea was my favorite grandmother. My grandparents partnered together in a cotton business. I spent that summer in their cotton fields, chopping cotton with my cousins Dewey Lee, Doris, and Darnetta Watson. It's one thing to read about the hardships slaves experienced in the cotton fields of the South or the difficulties people endured in the Mississippi Delta, but it's another thing to live it. That summer gave me an even deeper appreciation for my extended family on both sides. I have profound respect for generations of Black people who worked from sunrise through the heat of the day until late in the evening to survive.

People who work in the cotton fields wear long-sleeved shirts and large hats to protect themselves from the sun's rays. My cousins and I started our workday at 5 a.m. We rose early with my grandparents to feed the chickens and pigs before heading out to the field to chop cotton. Dewey milked Sue the cow early in the morning and did most of the chores. He was a hard-working teenager and well trained by Madea.

Madea prepared a hearty breakfast of biscuits, sausage, and molasses to sustain her grandchildren until mid-day. Around noontime, we took a brief break from working in the fields and ate lunch, usually under a shade tree. As tough as farm life seemed, the best part was that nobody worked on Sundays! Our African-American ancestors honored the Lord's Day and observed Sunday as a day to rest and worship. Sunday was their only day off from the demands of work. My appreciation for Sunday increased tenfold that summer. After a day of rest and worship, we returned to the fields on Monday morning.

The most challenging work was chopping cotton. Chopping cotton entails using a garden hoe to thin out excess plants and weeds around the cotton to leave space for the cotton to grow. This is hard work, especially when it's done in the heat and sun all day. I probably chopped more cotton than excess weeds, but my grandparents never pulled me from the fields. They let me sweat in the heat and learn what it was like to work hard and own a business.

They owned their land and had a pretty successful business. They paid their workers at the end of each day. I had volunteered to be free labor for my grandparents that summer, but when it was time to head back to the city, I got rewarded with a $20 bill and a new pair of tennis shoes. The tennis shoes were what we called "egg bottoms" back at Greenville High School, cheap tennis shoes that cost only a few dollars that could wreak havoc on a teenage boy's reputation.[2] I grew up wearing expensive Converse All-Stars purchased by my parents or

---

[2] Danny Dodd. Egg Bottoms. Personal Stories About Chucks. Date unknown. https://www.chucksconnection.com/articles/egg-bottoms.html

myself. All-Stars then cost about $10 to $12, depending on the color. When Madea took the "egg bottoms" back to the store and exchanged them for a pair of All-Stars, it made me feel really special. I knew she did this out of the kindness of her heart and a desire for all her grandchildren to have the best things in life.

Madea was a strong Black woman, an entrepreneur, and a caregiver who temporarily took a niece into her home during a time of family need. She knew heartbreak. Her daughter Lorean Watson, my father's sister, was tragically killed by her husband. That incident led to Madea raising Lorean's children, Dewey, Doris, and Darnetta. I remember Madea being loving but very firm with the grandchildren she raised. She rarely spanked me, but I recall one time when Dewey and I were younger, she gave us a good whipping for climbing on top of a metal shed.

Hard work carried over into my cousin Dewey's adult life and mine, although many would disagree about me being in that category. Dewey worked for a major tire distribution store in Memphis for over 40 years, where God elevated him to senior management. Dewey did not know how to read well, but he was an excellent people person, one of the best ever. He was like a big brother to me, and I learned so much from him.

My early years were shaped by the strong work ethic, entrepreneurialism, determination, and dedication to family passed down from one generation to the next. These values carried over into my relationship with Anita and my career in the military. I also benefited from growing up in a close-knit neighborhood of families who cared for each other. The other great influence on my road to manhood was the church.

Mom carried us to church every Sunday morning for Sunday school. Again, she was a woman of preparation. She laid out our church clothes pretty much the same way she did our school clothes. Dad stayed home and rested in bed after working hard all week and being at the club on Saturday nights.

Our church, New Mt. Zion Baptist Church, only had worship once a month on the third Sunday. There was not an abundance of preachers in those days. Mostly during this time, there were circuit preachers who served multiple churches in Greenville, MS, and rural areas. Our Pastor, Rev. H. A. Armstrong, was a large dark-skinned man and a kind and loving pastor. His wife was also super sweet. She sang in the Baptist choir even though she belonged to a Catholic church. She was very low-key, so much so that I didn't know her until I became an adult. Pastor Armstrong didn't oversee the church on a day-to-day basis. He mainly just preached. I can still see him pacing the pulpit during his sermon closing, holding his right hand on his ear, and heralding the Holy Ghost: *"I got a telephone in my bosom, and I can call God up whenever I need Him!"*[3]

The New Mt. Zion church building was moderate in size and furnishings. It had wood pews, two large gas heaters, and two large window air conditioner units. I remember it being freezing in the winter and hot in the summer. There was no teaching on tithes and very little on offerings. The emphasis was on church dues, selling raffle tickets, and cake bake sales to support the church. My mom was an excellent cook, so she supplied plenty of cakes to help fund the church. The money was counted upfront in the center of the sanctuary on a table for everyone to see, perhaps for transparency or because there wasn't enough money to worry about someone stealing.

Pastor Armstrong believed in order and respect. One deacon who acted like he ran the church tried to give himself a Deacon Appreciation Day, but it got halted by Pastor Armstrong. If anyone ever wondered who the leader of New Mount Zion Baptist Church was, they soon found out after the Deacon Appreciation Day was canceled.

I grew up in the days when the church had what was called a mourners' bench, sometimes called a mourning bench. This was a time

---

[3]   Amazing Farmer Singers of Chicago. (unknown). I got a telephone in my bosom. [Recorded by the Amazing Farmer Singers of Chicago]. (45 rpm). Chicago, IL: HLF Records. (unknown)

when during a revival, parents sat their children on the front pew of the church, the mourners' bench, and members would pray for their salvation and acceptance of Jesus Christ. Saints of old believed you could not be saved unless you felt something or had an emotional experience of some kind, and came off the bench crying and shouting. There was usually a week-long church revival where the unsaved would sit in the front row waiting to feel something, hopefully before the end of the week. I don't recall feeling anything sitting on the mourners' bench. I do remember my brother Andrew and me being there together. I don't know who responded first and confessed Christ as our Lord and Savior, but we both became candidates for baptism during that revival. Soon afterward, Andrew and I were baptized together at 11 and 12 years old, respectively. This was my public confession of Christ, and Sunday school played the most important role in my biblical teaching on salvation and belief in Jesus Christ.

Despite its moderate resources, New Mt. Zion was filled with love and excellent Sunday school teachers. During my early teenage years, my Sunday school teachers were Sis. Laura Super and Sis. Mandy Pope. Both were loving and extremely kind. During Sunday school reassembly, we stood before the congregation to share what we learned and memorized from the lesson. For many of us, this helped build our confidence in public speaking. When I became an older teenager, I moved on to the adult men's class led by Mr. Leon Stewart, a passionate teacher who was always well-prepared. He taught the word with authority and boldness, like a lawyer arguing a case. I also remember Ms. Lillie Bennett taught the women's Sunday school class. Ms. Bennett was also a strong, radical, and authoritative teacher who was not only vocal about her views on scriptures, but that the United States would someday pay for its sins of racism, discrimination, and social injustices. Ms. Bennett's teaching style was similar to a preacher denouncing sin and evil with a fire and brimstone voice regarding God's judgment. Mr. Stewart and Ms. Bennet were well-versed in scripture, and I admired watching these lay-persons teach the word of God in such a powerful way.

I developed close friendships with other students in my Sunday school class, two of whom became ministers later in life as well, Craig Pope and John Swilley. All three of us have had the opportunity to preach at the church that gave us the foundation for our biblical growth. I have a fond memory of Pastor Armstrong asking to see my preacher's license before allowing me to enter the pulpit, the first time a pastor asked to see it! During my early years of preaching, I kept it in my wallet, and it felt good to be able to show it to my childhood pastor when he asked to see it. After viewing it, he allowed me access to the pulpit, and I know he was proud to have me there. I'll always appreciate the New Mt. Zion pastors who gave me numerous opportunities to preach, including former Pastor

Wille E. Tinson, a beloved family member, and the love and enthusiastic embrace my family received whenever we journeyed home.

The church was a special place for my mother and me. I faced a dilemma when I was hired at Big Boy Restaurant. I was required to work on Sundays and missed going to church. I'd only been working there a few weeks when I asked my mom about quitting. She said it was my choice. She empowered her children's lives by giving us the freedom to make decisions. After her blessing, I promptly quit my job and was soon back at New Mt. Zion on Sundays.

African Americans in the Delta produced a vibrant culture that sustained them through hard times. The region produced the blues, a music that grew out of traditional work songs and articulated the sufferings of blacks and the way music could transcend them. The black church also insulated its believers from the traumas of living in an oppressive society. The one institution controlled by blacks under racial segregation, the church offered a sense of self-respect and esteem for people who rarely received respect from the institutions and customs of the larger society.[4]

This passage from *Southern Spaces* perfectly captures what I witnessed and experienced at New Mt. Zion growing up, the connectedness, love, protection, and respect the members had for each other. My mother served faithfully as Sunday School Assistant

---

4   Wilson, Charles R. Mississippi Delta. <u>Southern Spaces</u>, April 4, 2004. https://southernspaces.org/2004/mississippi-delta/

Superintendent and as an usher, and she always wore a neat, white uniform with an usher's badge. Ushers were treated with much respect by church members. I remember them moving through the church like sentinels, collecting gum from members who made the mistake of chewing it during the service. The Usher held out their hand so the member could place their gum in tissue and hand it to them. They were also diligent in handing out church fans during the summer months, providing relief to people sitting in a packed hot church. Whereas the worship was always on fire for the Lord in my small home church, it's the opposite today. Too often, we have large, air-conditioned churches and empty pews.

My worldview about God was shaped by Sunday school in those adolescent years. Learning how God moved in the lives of His people and rescued them in times of oppression was vitally important to me. The story of the Children of Israel's deliverance from bondage and how God sustained His people for 40 years in the wilderness was also dear to my mother. I believe this resonated with her because of her upbringing. I know the hardships of farm work heavily impacted her. She was a daughter of the Mississippi Delta who'd grown up picking cotton and witnessing her parents work extremely hard. She grew up knowing that African Americans, oppressed and mistreated by white people, wanted something better for themselves. She had great respect and love for her father, one of the most hard-working men I've ever known. Granddaddy Russell was only 64 years old when he died of a heart attack in December 1984. He lived an exemplary life and is still held in high regard by his descendants. When he passed, Anita was one month pregnant with our youngest son Marvin Jr., a symbolic moment of one generation passing and another entering the world.

My parents were good providers and disciplinarians, and we never doubted their love for us. Even so, my childhood wasn't ideal by any means. Emotional and physical boundaries were infringed upon in ways that were heartbreaking and painful to endure. I grew up in a home witnessing domestic violence, my mother being physically abused by my father. This bothered me a lot, even as an adult, ultimately affecting my relationship with my father. Domestic violence is a horrible thing for children to experience, and I believe it had a mental effect on all my siblings. We never discussed the violence in our home with one another. As children, we didn't know how to talk about being traumatized. We had no idea how we were absorbing, processing and internalizing the shock of seeing our father abusing our mother, or how it would impact us in the short-term or long-run of our lives. One of my brothers probably felt the same way I did as he became very distant from the family.

My mother was a quiet, soft-spoken woman. She never provoked my father into hitting her, and she never fought back, a smart move on her part. Dad was 6 ft 4, and Mom was about 5 ft 6. She didn't stand a chance in physical altercations with a man of his size. He usually became abusive on Friday or Saturday nights after he'd been out drinking. She would go to church even if he fought her early Sunday morning. She'd cook his breakfast, eggs sunny side up, serve it to him in bed, and then gather us up and go to church. If ever there was a person who lived out the scripture in MATT. 5:44, *"Love your enemies, bless them that curse you, do good to them that hate you, and pray for them which despitefully use you and persecute you,"* it was my mother. Her favorite gospel song was *Sweet Hour of Prayer* by Mahalia Jackson.

> *In seasons of distress and grief,*
> *My soul has often found relief,*
> *And oft escaped the tempter's snare*
> *By thy return, sweet hour of prayer!*[5]

Children who witness violence between parents may also be at greater risk of being violent in their future relationships.[6] I did not want to be like my father. I vowed never to hit my wife and I can honestly

---

5   Bradford, W.B. and Walford, W.W. (unknown). Sweet Hour of Prayer [Recorded by Mahalia Jackson]. On A Mighty Fortress (Album). Unknown: Originally released by Columbia Records (1968)

6   Effects of Domestic Violence on Children. Office on Women's Health, U.S. Department of Health & Human Services. August 18, 2022. https://www.womenshealth.gov/relationships-and-safety/domestic-violence/effects-domestic-violence-children

say I never have. Even so, witnessing my father abuse my mother did impact my relationship with Anita. Growing up, I wasn't exposed to effective conflict resolution in the home, which hampered my ability to communicate effectively with Anita.

I believe my mother stayed in the relationship with my father because she had five children. And although divorce rates started to climb in the 60s and 70s, it was still a rarity in our neighborhood. Among the twenty or so families on Abraham Street, I only recall one couple separating. I can only guess why my mother stayed, but I know what sustained her during those times - her faith in God, love for us, and sheer resiliency.

In 1978, I graduated from Greenville High School. My plan was to go into the military. There was a picture on the wall in our home of my father in his United States Army uniform, a distinguished image of him that motivated me to enlist. I took the Armed Services Vocational Assessment Battery (ASVAB) test. It was a customary practice during that time for a recruiter to visit your home when you took the exam. When the recruiter came, my dad discouraged me from joining the Army. He wasn't against me entering the military; it was just the Army, perhaps because the Vietnam War had ended only three years before.

He left the Army before the escalation of the Vietnam war, and it was a blessing that he didn't make a career out of the military, or he likely would have served in that war.

My sister Angela believed the United States Air Force was the top military branch and pushed me to consider joining the Air Force over the Army. The Air Force motto was "Aim High." As much as I tried to do just that, I failed the ASVAB test twice in my attempt to qualify to serve in the Air Force.

Since I wasn't going into the Air Force, I worked as a bricklayer after graduating high school. After working for a few days, I developed a hernia that required emergency surgery. I couldn't work for six weeks. While recovering, Mom took me to Morehead Junior College to enroll, several miles outside of Greenville. I was waiting to start classes at Morehead in the fall of 1978 when the unexpected happened. My beloved cousin Dewey came to visit us. He had left Shaw and moved to Memphis, Tennessee, to live with his beautiful fiancée Sharon Barton who later became Mrs. Sharon Watson. Dewey offered me the opportunity to return with him to Memphis.

As always, when it came to major decisions, I turned to my mother for her input on whether I should attend college or go to Memphis, and as she'd always done, she said the decision was mine. I decided to take off for Memphis with Dewey to start my adult journey in life. A huge factor in my decision was knowing that my mother was sacrificing to provide for her children. Being young and materialistic, I knew I would want nice clothes for college, and Mom would have to pay for things I desired. If I moved, I could forge my own way and not depend on her.

I was 18 years old when I left Greenville, one year younger than my father and two years older than my mother had been when they left Shaw to create a better life for themselves. Their journey had its ups and downs, but with hard work and determination, they established a solid middle-class existence for themselves and their children. I didn't know what the future held for me, but I'd inherited a strong worth ethic and determination from generations of my family, and I could feel God's hand at work in my life. Memphis was the right move.

CHAPTER TWO

The Military, Marriage & Back to Memphis

I visited Memphis for the first time on a school field trip in sixth grade, and it was my first glimpse of a big city. Moving there as an 18-year-old just entering manhood, I felt the joy of good fortune and the anxiety that accompany the unknown.

In 1978, Memphis had a population of over 600,000, more than 10 times the size of Greenville. Memphis is the largest city on the Mississippi River and the second largest in Tennessee. I wasn't just moving away from everything I'd ever known; I was moving to a new kind of place in a new state with its own history, customs, and traditions.

Fortunately, I had help getting settled in Memphis. My cousin Dewey Lee Watson, his sister Doris Taylor, and her husband Danny helped me quite often and treated me like a son. They allowed me to stay with them occasionally, and Danny helped me obtain a job at Giant Foods. Giant Foods was the major grocery store chain in Memphis in the 1970s, and the location where I worked on Elvis Presley Boulevard was the most popular store in the city. Although the store was down the street from Elvis Presley's home, he'd been dead for less than a year when I got there, so Graceland wasn't the mega-tourist attraction it would become when it opened to the public in 1982. Our customer base was huge, and it seemed like everyone who lived in Whitehaven came to shop in our store. During the late 70s, cooking meals at home was still more popular than eating out at restaurants.

I was working an unskilled job as a grocery bagger at Giant Foods and didn't have any long-term goals for myself. I was living a happy-go-lucky life. I had a car, but it wasn't reliable. I depended on my cousins Dewey, Doris, and Danny a lot. While living with Dewey and Sharon, they didn't inquire about my goals in life or how I planned to become independent. They allowed me the freedom to enjoy life while nurturing me to become responsible along the way.

Dewey had a tremendous influence on my life. I learned so many important lessons from him. He taught me how to drive a car and about sex and procreation. While he lived in the country with Madea, he enjoyed listening to Jerry Butler's song, "Only the Strong Survive." That became Dewey's motto and belief, that only the strong survive. We had many spiritual conversations about who he referred to as the "The Good Lord." He emphasized the importance of being honest and doing the right thing, lessons that would follow me forever.

While working at Giant Foods, I developed a close bond with a coworker named Terry Hardaway. Terry became my best friend in Memphis. I remember meeting his mother and how kind she was. We were similar in that we both had a strong work ethic and sought to please our supervisor and coworkers. We also loved to crack jokes and have a good time. We'd sometimes drink beer or go on joy rides in our vehicles after work. We visited nightclubs on the weekends. It seemed like everyone was dancing back then. I enjoyed dancing, listening to music, and just being in the crowd. We were young and living carefree lives without obligations, commitments, or significant expenses. During this time, I wasn't attending church. I had completely forgotten my Christian values. Thankfully the Lord kept his hand on me even when I was not thinking about Him.

It was the latter part of 1978 when, after work one evening, Terry told me he was taking me to meet this girl who had previously visited Giant Foods. I'd met a few young ladies in Memphis but never seriously dated one. There were plenty of girls in and out of Giant Foods, but I had no idea who Terry was talking about. He took me to The Treasury, a discount department store owned by J. C. Penney. The Treasury was about 5 miles south of where we worked. Life was so inconsequential for us back then that I can't recall what we talked about on the drive. I must have asked Terry how she looked or something like that.

Or perhaps we spent the time talking about which cashier had treated us badly that day at Giant Foods. Someone was always trying. Terri knew this girl because they'd worked together at The Treasury and attended Mitchell High School at the same time.

When Terry and I went into the store, he signaled to me the young lady he wanted to introduce me to. Her name was Anita Bachus. I may not remember what Terry and I talked about on the way there, but I'll never forget my first encounter with Anita. She was a cashier, so I entered her checkout lane to purchase something of little value just so I could talk with her. As I approached her, I stared at her beautiful face, which made her nervous, seeing how intensely I was gazing at her.

I was in her checkout lane, so I couldn't say much. I did ask for her phone number, which she refused to give me. After a few more visits to her workplace with Terry in tow, he convinced Anita to give me her phone number by warning her that I would hold up her checkout lane until I got it. When Anita recognized I was not giving up, she gave Terry her home phone number. Of course, there were no personal cell phones back then. The world hadn't transformed into the real-world version of the Jetsons cartoon that it is now. Anita was working, so we didn't talk much at the store. We just stared at each other. Honestly, I couldn't help myself. As we said back then, she was "fine," and I was very attracted to her!

We started "talking," the old school word for the first steps in a relationship, the phase when two people are getting to know each other and deciding if they like each other enough to start "going together." After talking with her on the phone, we started developing a close friendship. Then one night, I came by her job and offered to take her home from work. Her elder brother Patrick, who always picked her up from work, emphatically let it be known that it was not going down. I wasn't taking her anywhere. Patrick told Anita, "Get in the car." Since she couldn't ride with me, I boldly or perhaps blindly followed them home. Patrick sent Anita into the house and confronted me in their driveway. We didn't fight or anything like that, but we did have a peaceful conversation about his sister and my attempt to drive her home. To his credit, what Patrick did that day is what a good brother is supposed to do, look after and protect his sister.

During our talking phase, I made a few appeals to Anita to become her boyfriend, but she was already dating someone else. I wasn't dating anyone, so I asked her to quit her boyfriend for me, something she refused to do. I remember telling my cousin Doris how much I liked Anita and that I'd asked her to quit her boyfriend. Doris thought it was ridiculous and bold for me to ask that. I can be pretty relentless when I set my mind to something.

Dewey owned a sports car, a purple 1967 Ford Galaxy 500 with super large tires and a powerful 390 horsepower engine. It was a mean driving machine. Dewey would let me drive his car occasionally (he must have really loved me to share his ride). The car was so powerful I had to drive it with two hands to avoid losing control, which happened to me several times. I hit a few mailboxes and gas tanks at the service station. On one occasion, Dewey let me take his car back home to Greenville. My friend Terry rode with me. During a long stretch of Highway 61, I drove at 100 miles per hour. That high-speed driving could have killed me at 18 years old, but by the grace of God, I am still alive.

Dewey let me keep the Ford Galaxy 500 on some Friday nights. One time while the car was in my possession, I drove it to Anita's house to show it to her, and she fell in love with it too. On another occasion, Dewey allowed me to let Anita keep the car overnight, and she parked it outside her bedroom window on her parents' front lawn. I believe Dewey's purple Ford Galaxy 500 contributed to Anita turning her attention my way.

After working for Giant Foods for a year, I had a wake-up call. I was bagging groceries for customers, delivering them to their vehicles, and running price checks for cashiers on products throughout the store.

There was no future in bagging groceries. The job provided fun money but not enough for me to live independently. My cousins took great care of me and didn't push me out of their homes. Dewey and Sharon were patient with me, providing guidance, shelter, and love. For almost a year, I had been living carefree without any responsibility or a vision for my future. The wake-up call was realizing that my life was missing direction and determination, values passed down through generations of my family.

It was bad enough that I wasn't earning enough at Giant Foods to live on my own and that my life didn't have direction. I was also fed up with dealing with racism there from store managers and some of the cashiers. All of the cashiers were white except for two. Most of the baggers were African American. We worked hard at Giant Foods and tried hard to appease our supervisors. Even so, the managers repeatedly coached us on how to conform to work standards and directives we were already following. It was as though they couldn't see us performing well. One white cashier had a nasty attitude and acted like African American baggers were her little slaves. She often sent me to get her a drink of water. On one occasion, I spit in the cup out of retribution. I didn't make that a regular practice. Giant Foods was a wake-up call and my first direct, real-world experience dealing with racism. It was the inspiration behind my decision to take the Armed Services Vocational Assessment

Battery (ASVAB) test again after failing it twice. God's providence was at work in my life. He directed me to a military recruiting station next door to where I was bagging groceries.

When I went to the recruiting station, I met a nice gentleman who was an Air Force recruiter. I scheduled an appointment to take the ASVAB test for the third time. The number "3" has a spiritual connotation in the bible; it represents the Father, Son, and the Holy Spirit. After taking the test and waiting a few days for my results, I stopped by the station to check in with the recruiter. He met me with great enthusiasm, letting me know I qualified to enter the United States Air Force! After two previous failed attempts, I had passed the test! It was a surreal moment! I was in shock and elated! I had grown up watching television commercials featuring the Air Force's motto, "Aim High." By the grace of God, I was finally on my way.

In March 1979, I enlisted in the military on a delayed enlistment until May. I was excited about committing to serve in the military and having direction in my life. I would be leaving Memphis in a few months and didn't want to lose my connection to Anita. We were still just friends, but I knew in my heart she was the one because of her spirit, charm, and beauty. I could sense that she also liked me a lot even though she was still committed to someone else. I hoped that leaving wouldn't hurt our chances. She was there when Terry had a farewell cookout for me at his mother's house. Family members and friends came by to wish me well, too.

I was 18 when I entered active duty on May 31, 1979. The U.S. Air Force conducts Basic Military Training for enlisted men and women at Lackland Air Force Base in San Antonio, Texas. The flight from Memphis to San Antonio was my first-ever plane ride. When I departed for basic training, I only needed the clothes on my back. Upon arrival at Lackland, known as the Gateway to the Air Force, I stood in line at a facility to be issued military clothes.

Although basic training is intentionally rigorous, it's also a fun experience. I got to meet guys from all over the country. One of the first persons I met at Lackland was an African American brother from Memphis named Raiford Lomax. Because of our common background, we bonded like brothers. I appreciated him being there since most people in basic training were white. He was one cool and intelligent brother. We laughed a lot, had good times, and did our best to make the most out of basic training. We were part of a group of about 40 airmen called a Flight who were organized to function as a team. We were in Flight 414, Squadron 3723. The young men in our basic training Flight got along and performed well together.

I learned very quickly that basic training is a mind game to test your level of discipline. The rigorous running, marching, teaching, standards, rules, and regulations mold servicemen and servicewomen into a lifestyle of discipline, order, and respect. We marched in formations to various functions and respected the four airmen selected as squad leaders from our group. We attended classes together, slept together, showered together, and lived in the same open barracks. We did our best to respect one another's privacy even though there wasn't much privacy to be found. We ensured our underwear and t-shirts were neatly folded, learned how to sew, and made our beds with blankets folded at a 45-degree angle. We replied to our Technical Instructor (TI) with either "Yes Sir" or "No Sir" at the beginning and end of every sentence. We got up at 5 a.m. and went to bed at 9 p.m. After lights out, we talked quietly for a few moments until everyone fell asleep.

During basic training, no phone calls were allowed to family or friends, so I spent a lot of time writing letters and poems to Anita. We weren't in a relationship yet, but I treated her like she was my sweetheart. After six weeks, upon graduation from basic training, we were finally allowed a few phone calls.

The TI who instructed us during the first three weeks of training was away during the last three weeks. When he returned for our graduation, he was very proud when Flight 414 was recognized as the Honor Flight out of four flights. This was an honor of distinction, and we took pride in our team and the standard of excellence we demonstrated. This was the start of establishing high standards for myself in the military, which I would maintain throughout my career.

One of my souvenirs from basic training is a prayer I wrote during that time:

Dear God,

I say this prayer to You to help me make it through this day, to make me a bit more understanding, and even a little less demanding. I need the strength to fight, to always do what I know is right. And Lord, please teach me how to care when this world seems mean and unfair. Give me the warmth of companionship wherever I go so that, in return, my love for you can grow. Amen. - Marvin Mims, 1979, USAF Basic Military Training, San Antonio, TX

Another keepsake is a strip of black and white pictures that Raiford and I took in the photo booth at Lackland AFB. Unfortunately, I didn't keep in touch with Raiford after basic training. I started searching for him a few years ago and found his nephew, Michael Hayes, on Facebook. I learned from Michael that Raiford passed in 2015. After he moved back to Memphis, he had a son and three daughters and was a great father and man, just as he was in his younger days. I regret not staying in contact with my friend or looking for him years ago. The memories of Raiford and our times in basic training are special, a reminder of how short life is and why it's so important to stay connected with people.

After basic training, I received orders to attend Technical School at Sheppard Air Force (AFB) Base in Wichita Falls, Texas. I was assigned the job of Telecommunications Specialist. The alphanumeric code used to identify my specific job was 291XX.

In Technical School, I learned the basic skills to perform my job. The military provides in-depth training with outstanding instructors. I learned how to type on a teletypewriter and read paper tape. I had never used a typewriter before Technical School, but after just nine weeks of training, I could type 45 words per minute and decipher code on paper tape punched with an alphanumeric coding system. It's incredible the things you can learn with the right teaching.

At Sheppard AFB, we had more liberty than in basic training. We could go to the base club or even off-base. However, there were certain places we couldn't visit off base, like strip clubs or other venues where an airman could land in trouble. There was little chance of that happening since Sheppard AFB was in the middle of nowhere. My favorite memories of Technical School are enjoying the music of Earth,

Wind, and Fire, music that made me think about life, and celebrating at the base club during graduation.

After graduation, I was allowed to return home for a week before reporting to my duty station at Scott Air Force Base in Illinois. My family and friends were glad to see me in my military uniform, and I could tell it impressed Anita too. She was working part-time at First Tennessee Bank and attending LeMoyne-Owen College, majoring in Business Administration.

It must have been during that visit home when Terry and I spotted the guy Anita was dating at a nightclub. He was there with another girl. Somehow word got back to Anita, and she quit him. Now all of a sudden, I was the next man up and eligible. She finally decided to give me a chance, and we started a long-distance relationship.

My cousin Dewey had many conversations with me about having a strong determination in life, which carried over into my pursuit of Anita. I remember telling him I was going to marry her. He encouraged me to ask the Good Lord for what I wanted, to have faith in God. It felt good when I introduced him to Anita, and he told me, "You did good!" He not only admired her beauty, smile, and kindness, he was happy that she was dark-skinned like him.

The myth that whites are better than African Americans led to the belief that light-skinned black people are more beautiful than their dark-skinned counterparts. There is still a misconception today that light-skinned African American women are more attractive than dark-skinned sisters. The Black Power movement that emerged in the 1970s inspired new messages and images promoting pride in our race and the beauty of blackness. James Brown gave us new marching orders with *"Say it Loud, I'm Black and I'm Proud,"* and dark-complexioned women with magnificent afros stood out in television ads and on magazine covers.

Mom predicted I would marry a dark-skinned woman. She loved to cook and made cornbread two or three times a week, and I loved it so much I'd mix it with buttermilk and eat it by itself. When the cornbread was done baking in the oven, she would take it out and place it in a lower part of the oven so it could get dark on top. Because I loved cornbread that was burnt on top, Mom told me I was going to marry a dark-skinned woman. I always denied this because I liked light-skinned girls back then.

☀

Scott Air Force Base is about 30 miles north of St. Louis, Missouri, in the middle of cornfields. The base was the Headquarters for Military Airlift Command (MAC), which was the primary strategic airlift organization of the Air Force until 1992. I was fortunate to get assigned to one of the most prestigious Air Force bases during my first tour of duty as a young airman. I was amazed to see so many Majors, Captains, Colonels, and Generals working in the same building where I served. There were numerous commands on the base, large military aircraft, a credit union, library, club, bank, dental office, and hospital. Living on a military base was like living in a small city.

Servicemen and servicewomen were provided free food at the dining halls four times a day - breakfast, lunch, dinner, and a midnight meal. I feasted on my fair share of delicious meals provided by the federal government. Occasionally, I grabbed a midnight meal after work or on the weekends. Although I ate a lot, I didn't gain any weight!

I lived in a military dorm with a roommate, Will Allen, who outranked me. He was immaculate and organized, and I was just the opposite which required me to keep my side of the room clean. I was in a group of friends who gathered in the dorm every weekend to play the card game "Spades": Tony Aguillard, Tony Dozier, and a few others. Dozier and I were card partners, and we always made spectacular comebacks. We would play on the weekends from 6 p.m. Friday evening until 6 a.m. Saturday morning. Dozier gave me the nickname "Magnificent Marv" because of my card-playing skills. Aguillard gave me another nickname, "Cool Daddy." I was blessed to have genuine, long-term connections with these two Airmen. Dozier and his wife came to my installation as Pastor at St. Mark. Aguillard and I reconnected on Facebook after I became Pastor, and he has sowed bountifully into the Kingdom of God and St. Mark with tithes and offerings.

Military Police would come into our dorm rooms with canine dogs to conduct random drug checks. Some guys got caught using drugs and lost a stripe. To my knowledge, none of my friends used drugs; none of us got busted for drugs. I tried using drugs a few times before entering the military while briefly attending Draughon's Business College in Memphis. During a class break, a few older students offered me a hit on some illegal substance that sent me into a trance-like state. Sitting in class, spaced out and debating whether my mind would ever return to normal was scary. After about thirty minutes, I regained normal brain activity and was blessed to not have any serious damage. I knew from that experience drugs weren't for me; I was going after bigger and better things. I remember the time Jayne Kennedy visited Scott AFB. In 1978, Ms. Kennedy became the first African American woman announcer on a nationally televised sports program. She was also a beautiful actress. When she visited the dining hall, all of the brothers got excited! Celebrities did things like this as a morale booster for servicemen.

I worked as a telephone switchboard operator while I waited for my TOP Secret military security clearance to be approved. I developed friendships with women who had worked for years as telephone operators, and they would give me telephone patch connections from the military dorm phone in the hallway so I could talk with my mom and Anita. That hook-up was a huge blessing because long-distance calls by Ma Bell (Bell Telephone Company) were expensive, and Anita and I talked on the phone every night for hours. We talked about having a life together one day, getting married, and having children.

In June 1980, the National Baptist Convention USA, Inc. held its Annual Session in St. Louis, about forty miles away from Scott AFB. Anita came to the gathering with her family. This was a perfect opportunity for us to spend some time together after being separated for weeks. I traveled to St. Louis to visit Anita at the hotel. I don't know how we managed to spend time alone, but we made love for the first time in her hotel room. Our natural feelings for each other led us to do something we knew wasn't right. It felt right in the heat of the moment like it does when most young people face temptation. Weeks later, we discovered that our first intimate encounter had led to our daughter Takenya being conceived.

I don't recall the first time I met Anita's parents. Anita says I met her father when we were just friends, probably when I came to her house for a visit. Memphis is known for having a lot of churches, but I wasn't attending one then. I wasn't tuned in to Memphis' large and powerful faith community, so I didn't know Anita's father as a well-known preacher and highly respected pastor of a thriving church. Other than my being in the military then, I didn't know if he knew anything else about me, that I'd tried for months to convince his daughter to quit her boyfriend for me or that I was the one who had let her park a purple muscle car on his front lawn. I just remember him being a busy man.

I didn't know what to expect when I talked with Rev. Bachus about Anita. We were teenagers when Takenya was conceived, both of us only 19 years old. It would be disheartening for any caring father to learn that his daughter was pregnant out of wedlock at that age. As a highly respected religious leader in Memphis, it could have been a soap opera. I steeled myself, knowing I intended to do the right thing just like my cousin Dewey always encouraged me to do. Of course, Pastor Bachus was upset, but we had a peaceful conversation, and he consented when I asked for his permission to marry Anita.

Anita stayed with her parents for the first two months of her pregnancy. The pregnancy accelerated our plans to get married and start a family. It was as though it was destined for us to be together and for me to be stationed just forty miles away when the National Baptist Convention USA met in St. Louis. Despite our pre-marriage sexual intercourse, God worked all things together for our good; He turned our sin into good. ROMANS 8:28

Anita Beula Bachus, aka "Black Boo" and "Black Gal," and I married on August 30, 1980. Terry Hardaway served as my best man. We chose this date because it was the last Saturday in August and the pay date for the military, which gave us a few extra dollars to pay for wedding expenses. My mother, Peaches the Prophetess, who predicted I'd marry a dark-skinned woman, was thrilled to welcome a second daughter into the family she treated as her own. Family members and friends came from far away to attend our wedding, including my grandparents, who traveled from Shaw, Mississippi. I doubt Granddaddy Russell or my other grandparents had ever traveled that far from Shaw. One of my most precious memories is Granddaddy Russell giving us $30 in dimes for a wedding gift. I'm sure it was part of his savings. This was a significant act of giving since $30 during this time felt like $300 to us! I dreamed I'd hold on to those dimes as a keepsake forever, but eating is more important than sentimental things when you are struggling to survive.

A few days after the wedding, Anita and I attended a Bachus family gathering at T.O. Fuller State Park in Memphis, our place of departure before we left to start a life together. Anita broke out in tears when it was time for us to go. Leaving her family was very emotional for her.

We rented a nice new apartment off-base in nearby New Baden, Illinois. Because we lived off base, we received a monthly military allowance for living quarters to help supplement our expenses. The apartment was empty when we moved in. We used Anita's small savings to buy a bed, and my mother gave us a small 13-inch black and white television. Gradually we purchased one piece of furniture at a time from a store in Belleville, IL.

As a young married couple, our income was well below the federal poverty level, which, in 1979, was $8,414 for a non-farm family of four. My basic military pay in 1980 as an E-2 was $6,321. We had a used 1975 Chrysler Cordova. The car note was $130 a month with insurance of about $75 a month, so our vehicle expenses took a large part of my pay. Getting paid twice a month, on the 15th and the last day of the month, helped us make it from paycheck to paycheck, unlike the current system of once-a-month pay. Fortunately, while we were at Scott AFB, my dad always gave Anita and me traveling money when we visited home.

Once my security clearance was granted, I had an important job working as a Telecommunications Operations Specialist transmitting and receiving classified messages. I worked in what was called a COMCENTER, short for Communications Center. Our COMCENTER was a 24-hour operation with three different shifts rotating every 2 weeks. Working with classified messages and material is one of the most sensitive jobs in the military. Messages must be routed to the proper destination and released to the appropriate individuals. This required paying specific attention to detail while performing my job. I always sought to provide accuracy in all areas of message processing, which helped me get promoted to a unique position within the COMCENTER within a year. I was assigned to handle outgoing messages daily, which allowed flexibility in my work hours. I would work the peak hours from 1-9 p.m., and if I finished earlier, I could go home, which I frequently did. At other times I had to work late to ensure all message traffic was processed. This was my first real job in the military, and I worked with very little supervision. I was entrusted by the Superintendent of our Communications Flight with an important job, and I was good at what I did. This first experience was the beginning of a long road to excellence in the military and private sector jobs.

While stationed at Scott AFB, Anita and I faithfully attended Greater Mt. Olive Baptist Church in Lebanon, IL, led by Pastor W. J. Griffin. The members of the church and Pastor Griffin would be a spiritual source of strength for our family for three years. They treated us like family, especially Pastor Griffin and church member Mrs. Mary Louise Clark, with whom we still maintain a close relationship. Greater Mt. Olive was a small church with a friendly congregation, and it reminded me of New Mt. Zion, the church I attended growing up in Greenville. Sometimes Anita would assist as a pianist. We never officially joined or tithed, which I regret after growing spiritually in the Lord.

Of course, things weren't always smooth and rosy. Conflict is a natural part of marriage and any relationship. When Anita and I were first married, we did not know how to communicate our differences when we were upset with each other. We were young and immature. Of course, Anita's perspective on this is a bit clearer:

Anita Bachus Mims

"I think that some of our differences were based on the fact that men and women think differently. I would not want him to stay out late with his friends because I knew he would come back full of beer and pass out asleep when I would want to stay up and talk. Over time we learned to respect each other's feelings and be more considerate."[7]

When Anita was pregnant, her desire was for a healthy baby, and my yearning was for a girl. I was at work on a cold, snowy night when Anita called to tell me her labor contractions had started. She was ready to give birth! I drove ten miles in a blizzard of snow to get Anita from our apartment and bring her back to the military base hospital to have

---

[7] Personal Reflection, Anita Bachus Mims, 2021

the baby. Anita delivered our baby daughter Takenya Anica Mims on February 10, 1981. I jumped for joy in the hospital when she was born. We gave her a middle name close to her mother's name Anita. It was the greatest thing that ever happened to me other than our marriage.

Anita and I enjoyed the blessings of Takenya and treasured our precious daughter. I have always enjoyed taking pictures, and I have pictures of Anita being pregnant for the first time. Watching her made me appreciate the transformation of a woman's body before and after pregnancy. We took plenty of pictures of Takenya to have keepsakes and memories of our firstborn child. Shortly after Takenya was born, my mom came to Illinois to see her first grandchild along with my siblings. Anita's parents visited us as well to see their first grandchild.

In the Air Force, having a child qualified us for government assistance from the U.S. Department of Agriculture's Special Supplemental Nutrition Program for Women and Infant Children, commonly known as WIC. We received much-needed items like baby formula, milk, and cheese through WIC. There was no shame in obtaining those benefits, although it is unfortunate that those who risk their lives for their country have to live below the poverty line.

After living off base for a year, we moved into family housing in a trailer park on base. Anita worked on base briefly as a server at the

Officer's club to help with our family expenses. We began bonding with other military couples and some single airmen who hung out with us as well. We were like one big happy family, playing cards and celebrating life. I enjoyed the military lifestyle, especially the close relationships we had with military friends and church members. Those early years of struggling financially and living away from family highlighted the importance of valuing relationships over possessions. Those relationships helped to sustain us during one of the most painful times in our lives.

About six months after Takenya was born, Anita became pregnant again. During the latter months of the pregnancy, my mother kept Takenya for us. Anita gave birth to our first son, Travis Drew Mims, on June 14, 1982. We treasured having a beautiful, healthy baby boy. We were one week away from taking Travis home to Memphis so our family could see him for the first time when, at six weeks old, he tragically died from sudden infant death syndrome (SIDS).

Anita Bachus Mims

"The death of Travis Drew was shocking and confusing because he was a healthy baby. I remember picking him up because it was close to feeding, but he wasn't responsive. I hollered for Marvin, and we called 911. They announced his death before leaving our home. Crying and upset, we called my dad, our Pastor. He comforted us and prayed with us. We later

learned many things about SIDS. It was such a sad time for us. However, with the support and outpouring of love from our parents, family, and friends, and because of our faith, we knew God was with us. I remember keeping Takenya home a little more because I didn't want anything to happen to her."[8]

Anita and I were devastated. Travis was so young and our firstborn son. We had never heard about SIDS before. The horrible thing about SIDS is that it's unexplained.

Even as I write this section, reflecting on losing Travis is painful. Our memories are never erased, but God gives us the ability to move forward by faith. The Lord had a support team in our lives to help us cope with losing our precious son. Pastor Griffin, church members from Greater Mt. Olive, and our military friends came to our rescue. Our military friends fried chicken and had plenty of beer for us to bury our sorrow in. Mary Louise Clark from Greater Mt. Olive showed up the night we lost Travis. She saw that I had a beer in my hand and told me I didn't need that; I needed Jesus. This memory remained with me for years.

Anita's father suggested a graveside service, which made sense to us and proved better for us. We traveled home to Memphis to have

---

[8]   Personal Reflection, Anita Bachus Mims, 2021

the service at New Park Cemetery. The service was performed by Pastor Bachus, who was also pained over losing his first grandson.

We could only stay in Memphis for a brief period before I had to report back for duty. We did not seek counseling. We relied on church members and friends who were there for us constantly, allowing us to grieve and filling us back up with love and care. Many of them are still our friends today, including Tony Aguillard, Tony Dozier, Will Allen, Mary Louise Clark, and Pastor Griffin, just to name a few. We will always be grateful to them for helping us cope with such a painful loss. We also relied on our faith in God to see us through.

☀

During this time, I held the rank of Airman first class, an E-2 with two stripes. I was receiving excellent evaluations on my yearly ratings. On two occasions, I was submitted for early promotion by my supervisor based on my work performance. Being promoted early to Senior Airman was a sign you stood out. I was eager to get the promotion because the position offered significantly more pay and a prestigious rank for a young airman.

On both occasions, I failed to get promoted to Senior Airman, and I firmly believe that race played a factor in the promotions that were granted at that time. The Commanding Officer who made the decision was a white female, and every individual involved in the process was white. The second time I went before an early promotion board, I was told I did not receive the promotion because I had on combat boots. I was frustrated and angry with their decision because combat boots were allowed with our dress blues uniform, and the white male who received the promotion seemed overweight. Physical requirements were also evaluated.

I was considered a third time for early promotion to Senior Airman, but that time, I did not show up for the promotion board. Yes, I learned to boycott early in life. When my supervisor called my house looking for me, I didn't answer the phone. I was frustrated and hurt. The part of me that knew I wasn't just a good airman, that I was an excellent airman, didn't want to go through the humiliation of being told I wasn't good enough again. The news of my not showing up got to my Non-Commissioned Officer in Charge (NCOIC), a white male who ranked two grades above my supervisor. The white female Commanding Officer ordered the NCOIC to give me a letter of counseling, a formal way of letting me know that my not showing up for the promotion board was unacceptable. The NCOIC knew my work ethic and excellent work standards. He called me into his office and gave me the letter, which he regretted doing based on our conversation.

This influenced my decision to separate from the Air Force early in my career. Being promoted to Senior Airman would have meant significantly more pay for a young airman struggling financially to support a family. I didn't want to have to maneuver through a culture where race was a factor in my being promoted. And although Travis' death didn't affect my work, it also influenced my decision to separate from the military during my first enlistment.

Anita supported my decision to leave the military. Takenya was only 2 years old. I told Anita I had reemployment rights at Giants Food, although this wasn't something I was counting on. Employment and our living conditions were just two of the unknowns. People all over America were talking about Reaganomics, or "voodoo economics," as his opponents called it. It was a period of high unemployment, high inflation, and high interest rates, with decreased social spending and increased military spending. The poverty rate increased from 11.1 percent to 15 percent. Critics would point to the widening income gap, an atmosphere of greed, and the national debt tripling in eight years as proof that Reaganomics failed. In other words, it was not the best time to leave a guaranteed government job in the military, but we exercised faith in God again!

In 1983, after serving four years in the U.S. Air Force, I separated from the military. Anita and I had spent 3 and ½ years stationed at Scott

Air Force Base. After many hugs and well wishes, we packed up our little daughter Takenya and headed back home to Memphis.

Pastor Bachus and Mother Bachus were receptive to us staying with them while we searched for an apartment. They made us feel at home. Anita, Takenya, and I moved into the room that Anita occupied growing up. Her brothers Patrick, Rodney, and Timothy were still living at home. Mother Bachus cooked delicious meals for the family and took care of Takenya while we looked for employment and a place to live.

I went back to Giant Foods and spoke with management about reemployment rights, but sure enough, I was met with resistance. I didn't pursue it any further with the Equal Employment Opportunity office. Within weeks I was hired by RCA Corporation as a Telecommunications Operator at the Navy Base in Millington, TN. Anita quickly landed a full-time job with a local bank in West Memphis, Arkansas.

After two weeks, Anita and I moved into a comfortable two-level apartment in Lakeside Downs, an apartment community in the Whitehaven area of Memphis. It offered us convenience, being near Anita's family and our babysitter Mrs. Lena Hurt, Anita's cousin who we lovingly called "Aunt Lena." Aunt Lena was the babysitter for the Bachus family and many St. Mark church members. She ran the best home daycare in Memphis with strict rules and love for all the children in her care.

After living in an apartment for a few months, Anita and I connected with a member of St. Mark, Sis. Georgia Torrance, to become our real estate agent. Sis. Torrance is a highly motivated agent, and she did not waste time finding us a house to buy. In 1984, Anita and I completed a loan application to purchase a home with my Veteran Affairs benefits. The house was selling for $42,500, making the monthly payment $475.00. Our income was insufficient to buy the house we wanted; we needed an extra $125 each month to pay the mortgage.

I heard about the Tennessee Air National Guard and checked into joining on a part-time basis as an additional source of income. The Air National Guard (ANG) is a branch of the Air Force controlled by the state government, and it is held to the same standards as the Air Force and can be activated by the Federal government.

After being back in Memphis for a brief period, I had put military options on the table again. I did not want to rejoin the military based on my prior experience of failing to get promoted early in my career due to perceived racism. However, we needed the extra money. Those thoughts weighed heavily on me when I met the late MSgt. Harry Grubbs, my recruiter. MSgt. Grubbs was the ultimate professional. His kind and genuine personality persuaded me to rejoin despite my strong reservations. After weighing the benefits, I enlisted in The Tennessee

Air National Guard in Memphis, serving one weekend a month.[9]

Anita and I purchased the house and settled into our lives in Memphis. After losing Travis Drew, Anita was afraid to get pregnant again. She didn't want to bury another child. Neither did I. We waited two and a half years before getting pregnant with our third child, and my faith led me to believe it would be a boy. On August 2, 1985, Anita gave birth to our second son Marvin Bachus Mims Jr. We were filled with the joy of the Lord!

Marvin Jr. was a happy, healthy, and good baby. He smiled a lot and had a head full of beautiful hair. Sixteen months later, we had another beautiful baby girl, Tracy Ann Mims. She received her middle name from my sister Angela who we lovingly call Ann. She was very talkative (baby talk) and a happy baby like Marvin Jr. They were very close, and a lot of people thought they were twins. Our family was complete!

Our families have always been important to Anita and me. Growing up, one of my favorite cousins was my Uncle Jake's son,

---

[9] MSgt. Grubbs and I stayed connected on Facebook and remained friends after we retired. He constantly encouraged and inspired me in my community service. I sent him a message on July 6, 2021, about my autobiography. "Hey, MSgt. Grubbs, I am writing a book and mentioning you, the amazing recruiter who led to my decision to reenlist in the Air Force! THANKS, you are a great gentleman then and now!" MSgt. Grubbs' reply was, "Thanks, Marvin! It's good to have worked with you, becoming a friend and a brother in Jesus!" Regretfully, MSgt. Grubbs died before on August 10, 2021, before I finished the book. I talked with his widow, Mrs. Mary Louise Grubbs, about my book, and she shared how her husband told her about it and his influence on my life.

Kent Bruno Russell. We had great times together when they came from Kansas City to visit us in Greenville or our families gathered at Granddaddy Russell's farm in Shaw. Kent and I dreamed about starting our own families, getting married, having children, and living in the same city together. Our childhood dreams became a reality when Anita and I moved back to Memphis, and Uncle Jake moved his family there. Within a couple of years, both Kent and I had gotten married and had two daughters and a son. Our wives developed a close bond as well as our children.

We were blessed that Granddaddy Russell and my Grandmother Madea lived to see Takenya, our firstborn child and their great-grandchild. Anita was one month pregnant with Marvin Jr. when Granddaddy Russell passed in December 1984, symbolic of one generation passing and another entering the world. Madea lived to witness the births and childhoods of her great-grandchildren Marvin Jr. and Tracy. She gave Tracy the nickname "Babygirl." Madea's and Granddaddy Russell's farms are filled with rich memories for our family.

I was 26 years old when Tracy was born in 1986 - a married man with three children, a mortgage, and two jobs. I'd served my country honorably for four years as an airman in the USAF and was serving again as a weekend warrior in the Tennessee Air National Guard. As an African American man, I had experienced being judged and mistreated based on the color of my skin. I'd gone through the fire of losing a child. And through every critical decision, crisis and crossroad, God kept his hand on me.

My journey led me to develop a closer walk with the Lord through Bible study, worship at St. Mark, and guidance from Pastor Bachus. Since marrying into the family, I'd gotten to know him on many levels and grown to love and respect him as a husband, father, preacher, and my Pastor. The spiritual crossroads between Pastor Bachus and me began in April 1985, when he appointed me Chairman of St. Mark's Annual Men's Day Program. On August 2, 1985, our son Marvin Bachus Mims, Jr. was born and was lovingly given the family name after my pastor and father-in-law. That was also the year Pastor Bachus appointed me as a Deacon.

In many traditional black Baptist churches, deacons are limited to counting money or praying. However, the position of deacon in the bible is closely aligned with supporting the preacher, preaching, and teaching God's word. I knew biblically that I was called to support Pastor Bachus and St. Mark in those ways, always with great importance. I would serve in ministry under his extraordinary leadership for the next 36 years.

CHAPTER THREE

Maneuvering Military Roads

Serving in the Air National Guard would play a significant role in my adult life and transform my worldview. I developed long-lasting relationships with people from diverse backgrounds. I worked with a team on mission exercises, war simulations, and drills designed to prepare our Wing for deployment in case of war. We learned how to operate military equipment used in war zones and wore military chemical suits and gas masks for hours to simulate preparing for chemical agents and gas attacks. The chemical suits were very hot in the summer, and the gas masks made breathing difficult.

From 1982 until 1995, I worked in the field of Telecommunications Operations for private contractors on the Navy Base in Millington, Tennessee. In 1995, the base ceased contractor services with my employer, and for the first time in my life, I was facing involuntarily unemployment. It was a time of uncertainty. I was responsible for four dependents and didn't know where my next paycheck would come from, but I trusted God to provide for my family. I applied for unemployment benefits for the first and only time in my life. I wasn't embarrassed, as some people might have been in this situation because it was a benefit I had contributed to, a safety net for my family when I needed help.

By this time, I had served faithfully for eleven years as a part-time weekend warrior in the Air National Guard. During my first week of unemployment, to help supplement my income, I scheduled my annual two-weeks active-duty military training with the ANG. The 164th Communications Flight (my Unit) often traveled for two weeks every year to a nice training site. On this occasion, I requested to perform my two-week active-duty training in Memphis so I could search for employment. Miraculously, God was working behind the scenes in my life. His favor began to blossom into more fruit for me when a full-time Telecommunications Specialist in the Air National Guard resigned from his position. It was a rare occasion for someone to resign from an active-duty position in the Air National Guard. The vacant position was in my Unit, Communications Flight. I was a Telecommunications Specialist in the Air National Guard with 16 years of experience working in the military and as a contractor with the U. S. Navy.

While performing my two weeks active duty, a Senior Master Sergeant (SMSgt) named Harold Gaskins offered me the opportunity to serve as a temporary Computer Specialist in the vacated position. A traditional Guardsman (weekend warrior) was my Supervisor before my two-week training. Consequently, SMSgt. Gaskins knew very little about me or my work history, but I am sure he viewed my performance appraisals before offering me the temporary position. I had a thorough knowledge of Telecommunications Operations from a civilian and military standpoint. I was an expert in my field, knowledgeable in message handling, routing, and processing; computer operations; and switchboard operations.

I had been working in a temporary capacity for a few months and performing the job to the best of my ability when the position was advertised for permanent employment. I applied and was hired permanent full-time by SMSgt. Gaskins. I was thrilled and felt it was a blessing from the Lord for someone to quit a job at the exact time I became unemployed, a position I was well qualified to perform. That was nothing but God!

During the brief time I worked for SMSgt. Gaskins, we had a great working relationship. He would later be promoted to Chief Master Sergeant. Chief Gaskins was the epitome of the Air National Guard in terms of his integrity, service before self, excellence, leadership, conduct, fairness, mission focus, and care for his airmen. He passed in 2008 after a courageous battle with cancer.

The late Master Sergeant (MSgt.) Chenata Jordan encouraged me to apply for the job. She was employed full-time in Communications Flight and was also qualified to apply for the Computer Operations job. MSgt. Jordan was a longtime friend who treated me like a son during my tenure in the Air National Guard. She looked out for me and my best friend Cornelius Yates, and was doing it again when she encouraged me to apply. After I was hired, she trained me in some areas I wasn't familiar with.

During my employment search, I also applied for a Computer Operations position with a private company. I was also offered that job, which paid more, but I decided on the Air National Guard position because of the military benefits. Military service offered me the chance of a lifetime to serve full-time and be stationed in Memphis. I was ecstatic about having another opportunity to serve on active duty and the challenges and possibilities ahead.

I took pride in my work and knowledge of military rules and regulations and wore the military uniform with honor. However, when I became full-time, I was exposed to a different side of people I had not seen as a weekend Guard member. I knew racism existed in the military; I had experienced it myself. I was surprised by the level of racism African American men and women, including myself, were confronted with as military members.

I believed strongly in the core values of the Air Force, "Integrity First, Service Before Self, and Excellence in All We Do." These values were represented in the Christian values embedded in me as a child by my parents, grandparents, uncles, aunts, cousins, home church, and village in Greenville, Mississippi. My adherence and belief in these values led to several confrontations with Senior leadership during my military career. Over time I learned that just because military members cite these core values doesn't mean they adhere to them, especially in leadership. I witnessed military leaders place personal agendas and the pursuit of power, control, and promotion above doing the right thing. I saw the role that nepotism and favoritism play in white people being promoted to supervisory and management positions and, in turn, opening doors for their relatives and friends. I saw African Americans being limited to lower-level positions and how the belief that a good ol' boys network existed discouraged challenging the status quo. After being selected to serve full-time, it didn't take long for me to experience it firsthand. However, this time was going to be different. I was determined to endure every fight, challenge, obstacle, and struggle. I had gained wisdom from the Lord and had experience on my side, and St. Mark had empowered me spiritually under the leadership of my father-in-law, Rev. Dr. J. C. Bachus, and by the word of God.

In June 1996, Colonel Dexter Tutor became Commander of the 164th Airlift Wing. Airlift Wings are made up of one or more groups consisting of several squadrons that are usually commanded by a Colonel (O-6). Wings encompass both operations and support activities. The Wing Commander is the Commanding Officer in charge of all military personnel assigned to the Air Force installation under his authority. There are several subordinate Commanders under his authority who lead separate Units within the Wing and fall within his chain of command. The Wing Commander is responsible for maintaining a cohesive group of airmen working together to ensure an Air Force Wing is prepared to fight and win wars.

This promotion set Colonel Tutor's path and my own on a course of interaction. A few weeks before Colonel Tutor became the Wing Commander, there was a change in the internal organization within Communications Flight. SMSgt. Gaskins, the leader I respected and greatly admired, was no longer my Supervisor. Within weeks, my new Supervisor approached me about attending a two-week training program in Knoxville, Tennessee, for a new computer tracking system designed to monitor aircraft in support of the Air Mobility Command (AMC) mission. C2IPS, which stands for Command-and-Control Information Processing System, played a critical role in the success of AMC operations worldwide. I did not eagerly jump at the opportunity to attend the training class because it was during the summer, and I was coaching youth in the Frayser T-ball League. It was my second year coaching, and our team was enjoying a 10-0 season with only a few games remaining on the path to becoming undefeated champions. Our coaching staff had invested a lot of time practicing and teaching our players how to play T-ball, be the best in their position, and win! Some of the players' fathers were assistant coaches who could lead the team when I was away, but head coaches never know how players will respond in their absence.

Shortly after I learned about the training, my former Communications Flight Superintendent, Chief Master Sergeant (CMSgt) Doug Williams, came by my office and inquired about me attending the class. CMSgt was an African American male and a strong leader. When I shared with him my reluctance to attend, he pushed me in the right direction by telling me, "The more you know, the farther you go."[10] My Supervisor told me the training was mission-critical, so with that information and CMSgt. William's urging, I quickly enrolled in the class. Also, I heard there were discussions about a potential military promotion for whoever was trained first on the C2IPS system.

---

10   Unfortunately, CMSgt. Williams passed away shortly after that conversation. However, his words lived within me, continuing to motivate me to gain as much knowledge and training as possible throughout my personal life and military career. Both CMSgt. Doug Williams and MSgt. Chenata Jordan supported me when I preached my first sermon at St. Mark Baptist Church in 1990. I was grateful for their support.

The upgrade would potentially be a promotion to the rank of Master Sergeant, which is the first senior non-commissioned officer rank and directly above Technical Sergeant. This promotion would result in more responsibility, prestige, rank, and pay.

A few weeks after I was enrolled, my Supervisor informed me I would not be attending the training and that another co-worker would attend instead. Shockingly, I was dis-enrolled in the class. The co-worker was a white male. We were both Computer Specialists and Technical Sergeants and qualified for the training, but I had volunteered and was already enrolled. On a personal level, I had adjusted my family schedule to attend. The white male had been a full-time employee longer than I, but he hadn't volunteered to attend the training, nor was he enrolled.

I approached my immediate Supervisor and shared why I should not have been disenrolled. I believed the decision was unfair and racially motivated. I opposed the decision and appealed it through the chain of command from my Supervisor to the Unit Commander, Support Group Commander, and Vice Commander. After exhausting all means of getting the matter resolved fairly through these levels, I brought the issue to the Wing Commander, Colonel Tutor. He was my last resort. He advised me that he would investigate the situation and make his decision in a few days.

Colonel Tutor was immediately confronted with a case involving an African American male and white male contending for the same training, and senior leadership in the chain of command (all white males) supporting the white male. This proved to be an early test for him as the new Wing Commander. Would he support what many perceived as a good ol' boy system or do the right thing based on the Air Force's core values?

According to Colonel Tutor, he did his due diligence regarding the decision rendered by lower-level commanders when investigating the situation. He asked my Support Group Commander if he had performed due diligence regarding the matter from my Unit Commander. According to Colonel Tutor, "The Support Group Commander stated he had investigated the matter." He upheld the decision of the Unit Commander and informed Colonel Tutor he would be supporting his Unit Commanders.

I've talked with Colonel Tutor several times, most recently in June 2021, about what he thought about the Support Group Commander's decision. "One day Sgt. Mims was going to the class because he was qualified," he'd say, "and one day he was not going."

To get to the heart of the matter, Colonel Tutor asked the Support Group Commander two critical questions: (1) what had changed regarding my qualifications before enrolling in the class and

(2) what Air Force requirements had changed for the class since I had enrolled? The answer to both questions was, "Nothing had changed." Since nothing had changed, Colonel Tutor believed I should attend the training class. In his view, I had been given the platform to go to the class and had decided with my family to attend, and it was the military that changed its perspective on me attending.

The Support Group Commander may have regretted asking Colonel Tutor what he thought about the situation. "I see it as a leadership failure," Colonel Tutor told him. "The only question is whether you are going to fix it, or am I?" Shortly after that, I was re-enrolled in the class. To his credit, after Colonel Tutor's investigation, the Support Group Commander reversed his decision in my favor.

The action by Colonel Tutor was about more than his leadership or my willingness to take a stand against discrimination. It was about the Air Force's core values being upheld. All of the other leaders in my chain of command had the same opportunity to do the right thing, but they stuck together in supporting a decision that was wrong. Colonel Tutor's decision signaled to the Wings' leadership they could no longer conduct business as usual without being held accountable. This was a significant victory for me and other African Americans in the Air Force.

We were in the minority on base, but we kept each other informed about racial issues. Colonel Tutor's decision in my favor made news around the base pretty swiftly. Before Colonel Tutor became the Wing Commander, many African Americans did not push their complaints through the chain of command because they believed the good ol' boy system worked against them. Those in power would ultimately uphold the decisions of their white male counterparts. Colonel Tutor acknowledged the 'good ol' boy' system was alive and well, and indeed trying to take care of themselves. He understood those networks were present in every community, including good ol' girls.

Colonel Tutor successfully handled this early test, allowing him to gain a lot of respect and trust from the men and women in the 164th Airlift Wing, especially African Americans. We perceived a change in the base atmosphere and culture, with more inclusiveness and opportunities to celebrate our heritage with Black History programs and other events.

Colonel Tutor believed this decision contributed to him being a successful Commander. His viewpoint was, "If not me, who? If not now, when?" words echoed by U.S. Marine Corp 1st Lt. Travis Manion. In 2007, when Lt. Manion's parents asked him why he had to return to Iraq for a second deployment, he asked, "If not me, then who?" He was fatally wounded during that deployment after coming to the aid of his teammates when they were ambushed in the Al Anbar province in Iraq. The Travis Manion Foundation honors his memory by striving "to unite and strengthen communities by training, developing, and highlighting the role models that lead them."[11] Colonel Tutor led in a way that reflected Lt. Manion's powerful mantra. He went to church every Sunday morning during drill weekends, setting an excellent example for men and women under his leadership. He was an approachable Wing Commander, eating in the dining room with the airmen and going to the club after a military training day to interact with them. He would later be promoted to Major General and serve as Air National Guard Assistant to the Commander of Air Training Center (ATC). His ability to "do the right thing" led to an outstanding military career and exemplary service to the United States.

I was excited about my victory because I did not bend during a time of injustice and overcame a prejudicial decision against me. Anita was incredibly proud of me. Throughout this ordeal, she had prayed consistently for me to prevail. She got to know Colonel Tutor during military celebrations and events, and we became close to him and his wife. Major General Tutor recently told me, "When you are on the right side, things kind of work in your favor."

After the training class victory, my relationship with my direct Unit Commander turned sour, and he maintained a negative disposition toward me for the remainder of the time we worked together. I recall

---

[11]   Our Duty: Empower Individuals to Unite Communities. Travis Manion Foundation website. https://www.travismanion.org/about-us/who-we-are/

having a disagreement with him regarding a job he wanted me to perform after he was transferred to another Unit. I refused to do the job because it was the responsibility of personnel under his direct supervision. He wasn't pleased, but there was nothing he could do about it since he was no longer my Unit Commander.

The C2IPS training material was complicated and challenging to comprehend. I was introduced to computer language and terminologies I wasn't familiar with. I had to learn how to completely install system software and clone databases on computers. I thought about how embarrassing it would be for Colonel Tutor and myself if I failed the class. However, I had easygoing instructors who worked with me and helped me learn the material, possibly even grading me on the curve on some tests. Thankfully, I completed the course! When I returned to my home duty station, I was immediately assigned to manage the C2IPS system. The position didn't come with a promotion, but it opened the door for continued job growth. This would be one of many challenges I would encounter in my 15-year career while serving full-time with the Air National Guard.

Fortunately, I had formed a strong bond with my assistant baseball coach, Tyrone Taylor, and the dads kept the team playing at a high level while I was away at C2IPS training.

The Crossroads of Champions

In 1998, I worked for a new Supervisor, my third in less than 3 years, and a new Unit Commander. I had met with my Supervisor on several occasions to discuss being promoted to Master Sergeant and my eligibility for the position. During this time, a Master Sergeant position was vacant, and I was qualified to be promoted. I was having lunch with a few military friends when one of them asked if I had heard about a white male being selected for promotion to Master Sergeant in my Unit. I answered no. My friend also informed me the white male did not meet the qualifications and was denied the promotion. They had firsthand knowledge about this from working in the Human Resources Department. I didn't have any information regarding the situation and was blessed to have friends in the right place to share these details with me. When I returned to work, I asked my Superintendent about the situation. He told me he submitted the request for the other male to be promoted and that it was his fault the gentleman did not meet all the qualifications before his package was submitted to a promotion board. I challenged his answer, telling him we had always been told it is the Airman's responsibility to ensure they're ready to be promoted to the next level. I was shocked and angry when my Superintendent informed me he would hold the individual's package until he met the qualifications to be promoted.

On multiple occasions, when I inquired about being promoted to Master Sergeant, my Superintendent's response was always the same: "I will promote the best candidate." Two people already qualified to be promoted: my best friend, Technical Sergeant Cornelius Yates, and myself. I never spoke to the white male about the incident. He was a part-time employee, and we never had much interaction. I had always utilized the chain of command when I had to address issues of inequality. I appealed my situation to the top level by meeting with the Vice-Commander. The promotion meant significantly more pay and career opportunity for me. I was prepared to take on another racial battle, but I felt I needed help with this one, so I asked Yates to support me in my appeal. I explained my dilemma, and he agreed to take time off his job to meet with the Vice-Commander and me and try to get our Superintendent's decision reversed. I was not surprised he agreed to the meeting because we had been best friends for 15 years and our families were close. We joined the Air National Guard about the same time in 1984 and roomed together when we traveled out of town for active-duty training. He knew about the good ol' boy system on the base, but he didn't have to deal with it daily, just one weekend a month. It was covert on drill weekends when everyone was on duty.

Yates and I met with the Vice-Commander and shared our complaint. The Vice-Commander promised to investigate the issue. After a few weeks, Yates was promoted to Master Sergeant. The Supervisor who promoted him didn't interview either of us; he just randomly selected Yates. I suspect Yates received the promotion because I led the protest. The promotion would have benefited me more in terms of pay and benefits because I was full-time and Yates was part-time. Still, I was happy that we prevailed and one of us was promoted. We had prevailed. Two years later, Yates retired and I was promoted to Master Sergeant shortly afterward. Naturally, the rank came with more work assignments and responsibilities. My Superintendent had a man-to-man meeting with me and put the issue behind him. It did not become a barrier to our relationship or my work performance. However, my Unit Commander, the officer in charge, was very upset and retaliation was on his radar for me challenging the status quo. I made it a daily practice to document my work accomplishments because I felt I was being micromanaged.

In 2002, I was confronted with another race issue. My Supervisor had retired, and the job was posted in a way I was unable to apply and be a candidate. I addressed this situation with the new Wing Commander, Colonel David Burton. After he investigated, I was offered a promotion to Senior Master Sergeant. Although I did not get the Supervisor position, this was still a promotion in rank. "We are going to see green and blue, and not white and black" was Colonel Burton's philosophy as the new Wing Commander. Green and blue represented our uniform colors; white and black represented our skin color. This was a powerful statement as a Wing Commander. During a later conversation with Colonel Burton, he told me he did not admire my Superiors as much as me, and he knew I was in a tough environment.

For 13 years, beginning in 1996, I worked for a Communications Flight Commander who seemed racist and acted like a bully for thirteen years. I often felt he was trying to intimidate me and showcase his authority, power, and intellect. I was always professional, and at times he acknowledged my outstanding job performance in work meetings. At other times he outright sought to embarrass me. He promoted me to Master Sergeant, Senior Master Sergeant, and then Chief Master Sergeant, but they were promotions with no personnel supervision responsibilities. Under normal circumstances, a Chief Master Sergeant would be leading airmen rather than managing a program. I still had to maintain control and accountability of our Base Communications Security program when I received these promotions, which required a lot of time and attention to detail. Knowing my job and regulations like the back of my hand and being extremely good in my position made both my Unit Commander and the Wing Commander look good. Even when my Unit Commander valued my outstanding work performance, I felt my race was a factor in him restricting me from supervising people. In a nutshell, I believed he did not think an African American man was intelligent enough to supervise white people. This was the scenario until a major situation occurred in 2009.

During my Unit Commander's last two years of service, our base prepared for a Wing level inspection called a Unit Compliance Inspection (UCI), one of the single most important inspections the Air Force conducts. UCIs are undertaken to assess areas mandated by law, as well as mission areas identified by senior Air Force and major command leaders as critical or important to the health and performance of a unit.[12],[13] My Unit Commander expected the Communications Flight to receive an Outstanding evaluation. Our Flight consisted of about 45 employees, some of the sharpest communication personnel I worked alongside in the military.

Before the inspection, a young white woman by the name of MSgt. Lisa Adkins was reassigned to my section within Communications Flight to serve as the Wing Information Manager. In that role, she was responsible for coordinating with multiple Units throughout our base and training personnel on Wing Information policies and procedures. MSgt. Adkins was my first full-time subordinate. I learned quickly that

---

[12] Air Force Instruction 90-201, The Air Force Inspection System, September 27, 2007. 11.

[13] The Air Force Inspection System transitioned in 2013 from large-scale external Unit Compliance Inspections and Operational Readiness Inspections to a system of majority self-reporting. Maj. Robert Atkins, USAFR. "Air Force Reserve At Risk With the New Inspection System." 01-01-2016. https://apps.dtic.mil/sti/citations/AD1054683)

she had asked her previous Supervisor for additional help carrying out her job duties for years. I believe MSgt. Adkins was reassigned because her last Supervisor determined her job performance was below the standards for passing the Unit Compliance Inspection. My Unit Commander *strategically* placed her under my supervision so it would reflect negatively on my leadership if she failed.

A few months before the UCI, my Unit Commander rudely told me MSgt. Adkins's section was unprepared. I immediately re-positioned my work area near her office to ensure she received the maximum amount of supervision, support, and assistance in learning her job responsibilities. The situation was so serious my Unit Commander invested in bringing in help from another base to assist MSgt. Adkins to prepare for the inspection. The person brought in to assist her was Technical Sergeant (TSgt) Marilou Pampo. TSgt Pampo was assigned to the 146th Airlift Wing, a unit of the California Air National Guard.[14] She had a great personality and came with ample knowledge, expertise, and dedication to assist MSgt. Adkins and personnel within the Knowledge Operations Management (KOM) field assigned to our Wing. This investment cost the base a lot of money and reflected negatively upon Communications Flight, but there were raised flags about why it was necessary.

---

14   The 146th Airlift Wing is located at Channel Islands Air National Guard Station in Oxnard, California.

I had previously asked for additional permanent manpower to support MSgt. Adkins. I supported that request by researching the manning (staffing) level across other Air National Guard Communications Flights. The data showed that most ANG Communications Flights had two full-time people assigned to Knowledge Operations Management (KOM), while we only had one. Also, a second person was assigned to our KOM office at one time, but the position was transferred to the Support Group Commander's office. MSgt. Adkins was doing the job without the same level of support others in her position had.

As the time approached for the upcoming inspection, TSgt. Pampo was providing a great deal of help to MSgt. Adkins. A few weeks before the inspection, it was rumored that a tough, by-the-books inspector was coming to inspect MSgt. Adkins work. This inspector was a white male, but something happened at the last minute that hindered him from coming. The inspection team recruited another person to fill his position, MSgt. Maria Hughes[15] who was assigned to the 172nd Airlift Wing, a unit of the Mississippi Air National Guard.[16] When MSgt. Hughes walked in MSgt. Adkin's office, we were shocked.

---

15   MSgt. Hughes was recently promoted to Chief Master Sergeant in the Air Force.

16   The 172nd Airlift Wing is stationed at Allen C. Thompson Field Air National Guard Base. The base is in Jackson, Mississippi, at the Medgar Wiley Evers International Airport, named after Medgar Evers, the Field Secretary for the NAACP and civil rights activist assassinated in 1963.

We didn't expect to see an African American woman walk through the door. God had sent a guardian angel to watch over us, to keep us from the hand of the enemy. MSgt. Hughes was a people person with a cool personality, confidence, and expert knowledge in her area. Without questions, she seemed to immediately recognize a problem in our section and that it had been going on for a long time. It was as though she perceived the division in our section and the lack of support from leadership. When MSgt. Hughes showed up at the base, my Unit Commander told me I must have been praying a lot, an unfortunate statement that was out of line. My response was, "We have been working a lot, Sir, working to correct the deficiencies in MSgt. Adkin's section." I felt my Unit Commander was out for revenge against us, but God intervened."

I'm sure our Unit Commander was surprised when MSgt. Hughes graded the KOM section with an overall Satisfactory rating. While he was so focused on MSgt. Adkins's section, additional work areas in Communications Flight were also rated Satisfactory. He expected these areas to receive a higher rating that would boost Communications Flight's overall rating to Excellent. Because so many other areas received a Satisfactory rating, Communications Flight was given an overall Satisfactory rating, a blow to the Unit Commander. It was a blessing MSgt. Adkins's section alone didn't cause the overall Satisfactory rating for Communications Flight. Nevertheless, both MSgt. Adkins and I took a lot of heat afterward from the Unit Commander because he had nowhere else to take out his frustration, anger, and revenge.

The madness didn't end there. My Unit Commander called me into his office and demanded I give MSgt. Adkins an Unsatisfactory performance evaluation. I believed the intent was to take the first step in creating grounds for her termination of employment, which would also reflect negatively on my performance as her Supervisor. I refused to give her an Unsatisfactory evaluation. My Unit Commander called me into his office again, this time with another Chief Master Sergeant from our Flight as a witness. He demanded once again that I give MSgt. Adkins an Unsatisfactory performance evaluation and, again, I refused. The Unit Commander became very upset and accused me of failing to do my job. I was doing my job.

When I contacted the Chief of Base Personnel for guidance regarding this matter, I was informed that the Unit Commander could not order me to write an Unsatisfactory performance evaluation on my subordinate. If the Unit Commander disagreed with the evaluation, there was a section on the form where he could express his opposition to the rating. Unfortunately, when that Unit Commander retired in 2010, the new Unit Commander maintained the same aggressive approach toward me tracking MSgt. Adkin's work performance.

In 2011, after serving under the leadership of the new Unit Commander for a year, my annual extension for military service expired. I had reached the point in my career I could receive my 20-year military retirement and be honorably discharged. However, I was not ready to retire and desired an additional one-year extension for military service. My Unit Commander had three options: allow me to reenlist for a certain number of years, extend me annually, or deny my retention. He refused to allow me to extend for an additional year. I believe it was mainly due to the escalation conflict resulting from my refusal to write an Unsatisfactory appraisal on MSgt. Adkins. The shit hit the fan when I found out another Chief Master Sergeant (Chief) within our Unit had written an Unsatisfactory evaluation on MSgt. Adkins and given it to her to sign. I sent an inflamed email to my Commander denouncing the matter. And I still refused to write an Unsatisfactory performance evaluation on MSgt. Adkins. This was certainly the end of my military career. Standing on my principles of right and wrong made a difference and the advice I had received from Chief MSgt Richard Regel (Ret.) years ago echoed in my ear, "When in leadership, take care of your people."

Performance evaluations are done by the first-line Supervisor on their direct personnel. For another supervisor to write an evaluation of an employee under my supervision was inappropriate and disrespectful. Because I had vehemently opposed this matter, I was presented with Unsatisfactory and Satisfactory evaluations for 2009 and 2010, respectively, by my new Unit Commander. He didn't write the evaluations. The previous Unit Commander had left those unsigned performance evaluations as wildcards to use against me, a secret act I didn't know about until after he was gone. Those evaluations were considered significantly below my expected level of performance as a Chief Master Sergeant.

I refused to sign them. Instead, I met with the Navy Judge Advocate General (JAG) at the Naval Support Activity in Millington, TN, to get legal guidance on addressing the matter before retirement. The Navy JAG officer advised me that the two evaluations would be reflected on my record if I pursued employment with the Federal Civil Service. The JAG officer suggested I meet with my Wing Commander and let him know my intent to file a complaint with the Air Force Inspector General (IG) if the evaluations were not upgraded. Filing a complaint with the Air Force IG is no lightweight matter as this is a top-level complaint that civilian and military personnel can file with the Air Force. Typically, IG offices investigate cases involving fraud, waste, and abuse. The subject of a complaint can be a program or a person. There was no guarantee the Air Force IG would take my case, but it would have raised red flags for the matter to not be resolved through the chain of command since I had never received an evaluation below "Excellent" during my entire 32-year career in the military.

Following the Navy JAG officer's advice, I met with the Wing Commander and informed him of my plans to file an IG complaint. He requested I give him some time to investigate the matter. After ONE week had expired, I called the Wing Commander to find out his decision regarding my complaint, and he asked me to meet with him in his office. He presented me with two revised evaluations for 2009 and 2010, both of which were "Excellent." I was very pleased and felt the right thing was done to resolve all the drama that went down at the end of my military career. It was a relief that I didn't have to file a complaint with the Air Force Inspector General because the Wing Commander resolved the issue. If I had not taken this action, the previous evaluations would have impeded my ability to obtain future Federal employment. I was determined to not let my record be tarnished by those who sought to retaliate against me for confronting racism, adhering to the Air Force's core values, and "taking care of my people."

I often met champions in the community who shared similar experiences confronting racism in the military. On June 7, 2021, I traveled to 3rd Street in South Memphis to purchase buffalo fish from Kimble Fish Market. I met a man there named Danny, a letter carrier with the U.S. Postal Service. We started a conversation about our military service inside Kimble's that continued outside in the parking lot. When he asked me the rank I retired as in the military, I was proud to tell him Chief Master Sergeant. He told me he served in the Army but decided to separate after Desert Storm because of racism. The specific incident was similar to one of the incidents that happened to me. When he was in the Army, a white soldier was selected to attend a training class rather than him. He felt the decision was racially motivated and regretted getting out of the military based on that incident. I gave him words of encouragement and let him know he was on the same path to retirement from the U.S. Postal Service in three years. Danny also told me his son had been recently terminated from his job because he filed a racial complaint against a manager. The company previously told Danny's son no action would be taken against him for filing the complaint, but he was fired shortly after he took that step. We understood why "you have to pick your battles wisely" when dealing with racism.

A few months later, I met another gentleman who separated from the U.S. Army after 8 years due to racism and his inability to get promoted to E-4. He has owned his own funeral home in Memphis for years. Sadly, these experiences are all too common.

President Truman desegrated the military in 1948 (Executive Order 9981), almost 30 years before I joined, but it wasn't until six years after the order was signed that the U.S. Army disbanded its last all-black Unit. Despite the progress made over the years to create a more inclusive and equitable military, much of what I experienced is still happening. Nearly a third of African American U.S. military servicemembers reported experiencing racial discrimination, harassment, or both during a 12-month period, according to results of a long-withheld 2017 Defense Department survey that underscores concerns about racism in the ranks (Stewart, 2021).[17] This is unfortunate since black military servicemembers have served their country well and sacrificed their lives since the American Revolution. I am a firm believer our resilience makes us stronger. I also believe it's time to end racism.

☀

I was blessed to retire from the United States Air Force on December 1, 2011, as a Chief Master Sergeant and be awarded the Meritorious Service Medal. The Meritorious Service Medal is awarded to members of the armed forces of the United States who distinguish themselves by either outstanding achievement or meritorious service

---

17   Stewart, Phil. Exclusive: Long-withheld Pentagon survey shows widespread racial discrimination, harassment. Reuters. January 14, 2021. https://www.reuters.com/article/us-usa-military-civilrights-exclusive/exclusive-long-withheld-pentagon-survey-shows-widespread-racial-discrimination-harassment-idUSKBN29J1N1

to the United States.[18] I had wanted to remain in the military with the benefit of financial security and serving my long military tradition. I was earning a nice monthly paycheck while on active duty and didn't know how much my retirement pay would be. However, my retirement income was more than sufficient to provide for my family's needs. It took months to adjust to retirement after working for 33 years and meeting the daily challenges of a job, especially in the military. I soon focused on other passions. I volunteered as a substitute teacher in the Memphis School District and became involved with a local school coaching middle school baseball. Little did I know ministry would become a significant part of my life.

---

18   Air Force's Personnel Center, Meritorious Service Medal, https://www.afpc.af.mil/Fact-Sheets/Display/Article/421888/meritorious-service-medal/

CHAPTER FOUR

Marriage, Family & Mental Health
"The Man in the Mirror"

Our marriage has been blessed with four precious children, Takenya Anica Mims, Travis Drew Mims, Marvin Bachus Mims Jr., and Tracy Ann Walker; a son-in-law, Joshua Desmond Walker; and two anointed grandsons, Hazen Desmond Walker, my prayer man and strong man, and Addison Joshua Walker aka "Happy." For forty years, our marriage has experienced tests, trials, and triumphs, and our relationship remains the cornerstone of our Christian journey in life.

Having children early in our marriage did not allow Anita and I to spend much time alone. Yet, it gave us the joy of family celebrations, birthdays, and graduations. We valued going out to dinner every Friday with the children. One of our favorite restaurants was Po Folks, not because we were poor, but because the kids got to eat free on certain nights and the fried chicken was delicious! We recorded episodes of our favorite sitcoms and watched them as a family. One of our favorite sitcoms was The Cosby Show because it showed an African-American family in a positive way. There was a father, mother, children, and grandparents with real-life issues combined with humor.

When Marvin Jr. was about six years old, I got involved with coaching in the Frayser T-Ball Association. Anita and my cousin Gretchen Graham persuaded me to pursue being a coach with this organization. I got my start from a white friend, a head coach who recommended me to the Association and opened the door for me to organize a team. I was the first black Coach to organize a team in the Association. Most teams only had one or two black players, if any. I recruited players from our church, family, and my neighborhood to participate. This became our family's life, purpose, and passion: to practice baseball and play games. This was what we lived for during the spring, summer, and fall months, connecting families together in the community and bonding young men together through our fellowships. This led to me organizing little league baseball teams with the Memphis Park Commission League.

When I started coaching, it brought me joy, and I found a special purpose in working with young African American males and their parents. I had been coaching for quite a few years with Tyrone Taylor when several mothers inquired about us providing additional support programs for their children beyond baseball season. We established a nonprofit organization to provide that support. In September 2001, we founded Brothers Offering Leadership Development (BOLD Brothers) as a mentoring program for young men to develop their leadership skills. Several men helped us establish the organization, including Patrick Bachus, Anita's oldest brother, who is a lifelong board member. Although we focus on building confidence, respect, leadership, and unity among young African-American males, we have also provided service to young ladies. BOLD Brothers partnered with St. Mark to provide Microsoft Applications training to both young men and ladies ages 9 to 17.

BOLD Brothers established community service as a key component of our organization. Shortly after the organization was founded, my search for service opportunities led me to the Metropolitan Interfaith Association (MIFA). MIFA was founded in 1968 after the assassination of Dr. Martin Luther King Jr. when a group of religious organizations came together to find a solution to poverty and racial division in Memphis.

Initially, BOLD Brothers started delivering food to senior citizens on Saturday mornings. Soon afterward, we got involved with MIFA's Christmas Day Meals program, which allows us to provide special holiday meals, gifts, and some cheer to senior Meals on Wheels recipients. According to MIFA, in some cases, the volunteer delivering their meal is the only person a senior sees on a holiday when they should be surrounded by family.[19]

I have enjoyed volunteering with MIFA for two decades. My volunteer service with MIFA was featured in the Winter 2021 issue of their publication Hope in Action.

"One of his favorite memories of delivering meals throughout the years was visiting a blind minister named Elder Futch, who died last year. "I would have fun with him trying to disguise who I was, but he knew me by my handshake," Rev. Mims says. They always delivered his meal last so they could stay and visit, often for half an hour or longer. He and his wife became like family to Rev. Mims, who took his own children on deliveries and appreciated the wisdom and positivity Elder Futch offered them. "MIFA connected us with wonderful senior citizens in Memphis, like Elder Futch, who gave us a lifetime of memories," he says.[20]

Our church life was integrated into our family life. Due to our love for the Lord and St. Mark, and our commitment to Pastor Bachus' ministry, most of our time as a family was rooted in going to church and spending it at St. Mark day and night. We faithfully attended bible

---

[19] "The Greatest Gift." Hope in Action, a publication of the Metropolitan Interfaith Association (Memphis, TN), Winter 2021, Vol. 40, No. 4, p.5. https://assets.speakcdn.com/assets/2161/hia_winter_2021.pdf?1635363248494

[20] ""

study, religious activities, church fellowships, revivals, and many other Christian engagements.

I was strict in raising our children to shield them from a worldly environment. There were certain television networks our children were not permitted to watch, like MTV and VH1. They couldn't watch television on Wednesday nights. Instead, they used that time for reading and studying. We didn't allow them to participate in Halloween activities. Takenya, Marvin Jr., and Tracy often share that I give our grandson Hazen opportunities to do things they were not allowed to do, such as participate in Halloween activities. We even let him hang a Halloween sign in our yard. I told them that parents learn later in life some things are not so important. Being religious can cause people to be legalistic and overly rigid with rules and regulations. This is just the opposite of Christianity. The religious leaders of Jesus' day were strict and had a lot of laws they implemented for others that they did not obey themselves. Jesus warned the crowds and disciples about the scribes and Pharisees. MATT 23: 1-6. Christianity doesn't constrain us from hanging Jack-o-Lanterns and enjoying sweets with our grandchildren.

Growing up, I did not travel beyond forty miles outside my hometown with my parents except on one occasion when I visited Uncle Jake and his family in Kansas. Anita and I prioritized taking our children on vacations to Florida, South Carolina, Hawaii, and many other places. My military service also required me to travel to military installations nationwide for training and mission exercises. Of course, the military incurred the expenses for those trips. In the latter part of my military career, I served as an advisor to the Communications Security (COMSEC) Unit of the Channel Islands Air National Guard in Oxnard, CA. I had developed close contact with a Senior Non-Commissioned Officer (NCO) in their Unit, and she needed assistance in passing an inspection they had failed. On several occasions, the Senior NCO and Commander requested my expertise to oversee and inspect their account. Anita would fly to California, and we would hang out together, spending time sightseeing and touring Malibu. We would also visit with family in Southern California and enjoy the beautiful beaches. Years later, we took our three children to California for a summer vacation and had a great time site seeing and shopping.

    Our marriage has not been a bed of roses. In any relationship, there will be conflict and obstacles to overcome. It took us a while to learn the scripture of not letting the sun go down on our wrath. EPHESIANS 4:26 However, as you mature in your relationship, you learn to pick your battles wisely and not allow everything to upset you. That requires knowing when to surrender as Jesus did, compromise by both parties, and knowing when to keep your mouth shut, which is the most difficult challenge in marriage. We often think we have to get the last word in and that this determines the winner! In reality, the person who *surrenders* the last word is the winner. Marriage also requires you to maintain a sense of humor.

Anita knows I love to make her laugh, and it keeps the joy in the relationship. My quick wit stems from my childhood. Growing up, my best friend Terry Sibley and I always played pranks on one another, and he was always ready with a quick comeback. With Anita, when she told me I was wrong about something, my reply would be, "You like telling me I'm wrong." When she told me I was right about something, my reply would be, "I'm always right." She would say, "Yeah, right." Anita and our daughters accuse me of being "petty" when I'm being sarcastic, shoot quick comebacks or dwell on minor issues. It's just my way of being me.

Anita's perspective:

"*Marvin would not give a person credit if they strategically beat him at anything. He always called it luck, except when he was winning,* **then** *it was because he was a genius. He did it so much that many thought he was a sore loser. We felt he thought no one had a brain but him. Not so!*"[21]

Unfortunately, Anita has modeled my competitive nature with recreational activities such as ping pong, shooting pool, and playing

---

21   Personal reflection. Anita Bachus Mims, 2021

cards. This is not a good feeling when I'm on the losing side of those activities!

After becoming a part of the Bachus family, I saw that Pastor Bachus was always full of humor and loved telling jokes, even in his preaching. I tried to imitate him in those areas but never developed the gift of remembering jokes. That has probably contributed to me using sarcasm in many of my conversations, sometimes to the extreme of insulting others. It's always in love, though! Growing up, I enjoyed television shows with positive African American male leads who had a great sense of humor. My favorites were *Good Times, The Jeffersons,* and *Sanford and Son*. These actors had dry humor like my own.

☀

Conflict is a natural part of marriage and any relationship. Over time, Anita and I grew in our marriage and learned to communicate more effectively. I attribute my growth and better communication to the mental health counseling I have received over the years. Since 2015, I have received counseling focused on my military career and how it has impacted other areas of my life from professional counselors with the Department of Veteran Affairs (VA). My counselors, Dr. Kim Fleming and Dr. Agnes Elder, helped me understand how the military shapes our personality and impacts our relationships with family in so many ways.

They helped me in my relationship with Anita and in dealing with my conflict resolution issues. During numerous counseling sessions with Dr. Elder, I learned that when you are in leadership in the military, you expect subordinates to obey your orders and not question your authority. When someone is programmed with chain of command authority, they need to be deprogrammed to function well in their relationships with their spouse and family. Because I wasn't deprogrammed, when Anita questioned my decision-making and authority, I processed it from a military viewpoint as being disrespectful or a lack of submission. It was difficult for me to process and respond positively. That led to communication problems and frustration in our relationship.

This is how counseling opened my eyes in my marriage and interactions with others. Dr. Fleming offered me long-term counseling, which benefited me in so many other areas: extended family issues, inheriting the leadership at St. Mark, and how to navigate through family and church drama. My counselors introduced behavioral techniques that helped me transform my thinking and actions, and gain a deeper understanding of life experiences. The model that helped me the most involves taking four steps: (1) observing my actions, (2) analyzing what I observed, (3) strategizing an action plan, and (4) taking action to improve my behavior. Using this technique, I've been able to communicate better, resolve conflict better, and promote my well-being.

I also participated in group therapy sessions with the Memphis VA. Cognitive-Behavioral Group Counseling is an effective approach to reducing anxiety in individuals. Not only did I receive help, but I was also instrumental in helping others in my group. I learned how many African-American males who served in the military had common experiences and issues usually involving racism.

Unfortunately, for decades many African-Americans were not offered professional counseling for the racism they had to navigate in the military during peacetime and while defending their country in wars that left them with external wounds and internal scars. Many who experienced nightmares and flashbacks of being in war zones never received the mental health counseling and financial resources needed to cope and heal. These struggles were intensified with the Vietnam war. Veterans of all races didn't receive a warm and patriotic welcome when they returned home because many Americans did not support that war. African-Americans served disproportionately in the Vietnam War. While comprising 11% of the U.S. population in 1967, African-Americans were 16.3% of all draftees, less than 2% of draft board members, only 5% of Army officers (2% of officers across all branches), and 24% of troops assigned to combat units.[22] While African American

---

22   Black History and The Vietnam, a Story. Tue, 06.20.1967. African American Registry. https://aaregistry.org/story/black-history-in-the-vietnam-war-a-brief-story/

soldiers were discouraged and, in some cases, prohibited from displaying posters or other images that showcased Black Pride, Da Nang Air Base flew the confederate flag for three days after Martin Luther King Jr.'s assassination. Confederate flags and icons were commonly painted on jeeps, tanks, and helicopters; bathroom graffiti proclaimed that African Americans, not the Vietnamese, were the real enemy.[23] Racial tensions escalated into protests, strikes, riots, and soldiers deserting their posts out of frustration with being treated unfairly. These were extremely heavy burdens for African American soldiers to endure without having access to resources to help them cope.

According to the World Health Organization (WHO), in 2019, 1 in 8 people, or 970 million people around the world, were living with a mental disorder, with anxiety and depressive disorders the most common.[24] Over 16% of African-Americans reported having a mental illness in a 2018 study, with less than a third of those receiving appropriate treatment. Stigmas and complex social issues remain significant barriers to mental health wellness among Black Americans. My seeking treatment for mental health will be seen by many as a sign of weakness. That's not the case, but I understand why it is still perceived that way. As descendants of slaves who endured 400 years of

---

[23] ""

[24] World Health Organization Fact Sheet on Mental Disorders. June 8, 2022. https://www.who.int/news-room/fact-sheets/detail/mental-disorders

bondage without therapy, shouldn't free-born African American men like myself have the physical, emotional, and mental strength to deal with whatever comes our way? That thinking is too heavy of a burden to carry. Fortunately, we are becoming more comfortable placing our history in perspective so it doesn't limit our current reality.

I'm also a minister. There are many reasons why the Black church and Black preachers, in particular, must address the elephant in the room regarding mental health. The Black church traditionally has been the place for holistic ministry for African-Americans, especially women. However, the church has to be more intentional in directing members to seek professional mental help when needed for their well-being. The power of the word of God has mistakenly led many faith leaders to preach that the gospel will solve all their problems. Consequently, many Christians suffer in silence. They experience an emotional high on Sunday but awake on Monday still depressed and struggling with the same mental health problems they've had for months or years. Seeking counseling from mental health experts should never be viewed as being unfaithful.

Black preachers and churches can't afford to continue treating mental health problems as taboo or be silent on the benefit of mental health treatment. We must prioritize educating members about mental wellness and advocate for them not to be ashamed to seek help when they feel overwhelmed with life, especially if they are suicidal.

Leading a congregation can be stressful, so it's wise for pastors to seek mental health counseling when needed and share the benefit of that counseling with their members. I have personally suffered from depression and was blessed to have multiple psychiatrists introduce coping strategies and techniques to help me overcome my depression. Those strategies included mediation, relaxation, regular exercise, sports, communication, community involvement, and adequate sleep. These activities have positively impacted my mental well-being over the last several years. Several times, I addressed the benefit of seeking mental health treatment while teaching and preaching the gospel. Almost every time someone in the congregation shared with me or another member how thankful they were that I addressed this subject. Young adults have requested personal counseling from me when I addressed mental health issues during my preaching, and one person admitted feeling isolated and suicidal. I believe talking about mental health during my sermons helped strengthen and save lives.

Recently we've witnessed world-class athletes like Olympic Gold Medalist Simone Biles and tennis star Naomi Osaka step away publicly from their sport to take care of their mental health. Famed actress and Howard University graduate Taraji P. Henson is a strong advocate for mental health. In 2018, she founded the Boris L. Henson Foundation, named after her father. According to Ms. Henson, her father "fought in

The Vietnam War for our country, returned broken, and received little to no physical and emotional support."[25] The foundation is dedicated to eradicating the stigma around mental health issues in the African-American community. I hope we will continue chipping away at those stigmas so we can embrace mental health counseling and improve our overall well-being.

A good friend, Barbara Pruitt, has been another loyal counselor to our family for years. I am grateful to her for helping bridge the divide between our daughter Takenya and myself. Takenya sensed that we loved Tracy and Marvin Jr. more than her because of how we treated her growing up. The counseling with Barbara helped us break through communication barriers and helped Takenya understand she was not loved any less, that with time parents grow in their parenting skills. Takenya came to understand we made changes to our parenting style and, most importantly, parents are not perfect. I was able to express to Takenya that we grew as parents in raising her siblings, but with her being our first child, we needed time and experience to learn how to parent. I confessed as a father that I was not perfect, but I perfectly loved her and only wanted the best for her. I acknowledged years later that my parenting style was overbearing for her personality.

---

[25] A Letter from the Founder (Taraji P. Henson). Boris L. Henson Foundation. July 12, 2022. https://borislhenson.wpengine.com/a-letter-from-the-founder/

It was only through counseling that I realized the need to accept Anita for the beautiful, unique, and gifted woman God created her to be rather than someone to conform to my likeness. In the words of one of my VA counselors, if God wanted two people like me, He would have made two. Through counseling, I began to acknowledge the fact Anita was not the one who needed to change; I needed to change. This reminds me of my favorite musical artist Michael Jackson and the lyrics from his song *Man in the Mirror:* "I'm starting with the man in the mirror, I'm asking him to change his ways."[26]

Marriage is a journey, and I am blessed to share that journey with a phenomenal partner. Along the way, I've enjoyed helping Anita reach her goals. Shortly after Takenya was born, Anita wanted to finish her degree, and I supported her 100 percent. She attended classes in the evenings so I could babysit when I got home from work. She was diligent in completing the requirements, and within 18 months, she earned an Associate degree in Business Administration from Belleville Area College (Belleville campus of Southwestern Illinois College). We struggled at times, but when we worked together to accomplish something, we usually succeeded.

I remember surprising Anita with a brand-new car. During the first five years of our marriage, we shared a car. She wanted and needed

---

26   Ballard, G. and Garret, S. (1987) Man in the Mirror. [Recorded by Michael Jackson]. On Bad (Album). Los Angeles, CA: Epic Records. (1988)

one of her own, so right before the birth of our second daughter Tracy Ann, I surprised her with a brand-new Ford Taurus, her first new car. I made sure it was blue, her favorite color. That surprise really made her happy! I've supported her in other ways, including helping her prep for interviews during her 36-year career with the government. I would give her advice and point out areas where she excelled, like conflict resolution and persistence in accomplishing assigned tasks.

Anita has always believed in my dreams and supported me in all my endeavors. In 2019, when I organized and planned a trip to South Africa, Anita was there to offer support. And that time around, she traveled with me! When I coached our son Marvin Jr., and other youth in little league baseball for St. Mark, Anita was there assisting by being a scorekeeper. She was great! She made sure the score was always accurate and helped us win many games because she would not let others cheat us out of our runs or allow the opposing teams to credit themselves with unearned runs. Anita helped finance and support Bruno's Italian Restaurant. She helped me launch BOLD Brothers and has volunteered with us for 20 years in delivering meals to senior citizens through our partnership with the Metropolitan Interfaith Association. She has assisted in serving meals in the extreme heat and cold to homeless people in South Memphis. When we had community meals at the church, Anita was always on the front-line serving and welcoming strangers into the house of the Lord. She provided service to families in Foote Homes and other underserved areas and has always shown the love of Christ while embracing men, women, and children in the community. Her encouraging words and friendly smile have brought joy to many.

Anita's outreach to young women has been exceptional. After BOLD Brothers was founded, she started BOLD Sisters and recruited ladies to support her efforts to mentor young girls. Her dear friends Renee' Brassfield and Lisa Dillard have been an anchor for her. When St. Mark sponsored block parties for inner city families, Anita was there serving and assisting single mothers and their daughters by providing personal hygiene items and clothing. Sometimes when women needed clothing, she would purchase the items with her own funds. She led a Women's conference at the Holiday Inn that gave women an opportunity to share their life stories. She embraces women who connect with our ministry, especially young ladies, teaching them Christian virtues and how to conduct themselves.

Anita learned faithfulness and commitment from years of observing her dear mother support her father. As a small child, she watched her mother be a stay-at-home mom and take care of the family while her father labored and served as a hardworking pastor. For decades, Anita saw her mother being a faithful servant to St. Mark as an awesome First Lady. First Lady is an unofficial term for the pastor's wife in many African American churches. Anita observed her mother being a humble servant who attended bible study and was involved with the church choir. Anita's path has been different as a professional working outside the home. Still, like Mother Bachus, she is a faithful servant and committed First Lady who enjoys ministering to the community and those in need.

Our marriage was made stronger by helping others, focusing on other people's needs, and spending less time on our wants. While doing ministry, we didn't dwell on our struggles. We kept working to grow the church, always connecting with people and inviting them to be a part of what we were doing. Working together sets a positive example for others, especially children. Recognizing God equipped and called us to be a blessing to those in need gives us a sense of gratitude.

☀

In 2013, Tracy and her husband Joshua gave birth to our first grandchild Hazen Desmond Walker. Ten months after Hazen was born, they decided to move to Houston, Texas, where Takenya and Marvin Jr. were already living. Anita and I were shocked. After waiting years to have a grandchild, all of a sudden, he would live hundreds of miles away! Since I was retired and Anita had been on her job for years and had plenty of leave to take time off work, we decided to travel to Texas frequently to visit our children and grandson. We hit the road almost every holiday and whenever we wanted.

I have a special relationship with Hazen. I call him my "strong man" because he has a strong will and personality, and is determined to accomplish things, often without assistance. We let him know it is alright for people to help him. He is a Lego builder and will stay on task to complete a complex 500-piece Lego set until it is done, sometimes late into the night. He was blessed with this gift from his dad, Joshua, and Joshua's father. He plans to be an architect.

I also call him my "prayer man." Our daily practice of praying together every morning and often at night has led to Hazen interceding on behalf of family members and others for healing. He prays at church and on the phone for family and people who are hospitalized and blesses the food at dinner. People are uplifted in the spirit and healed by his prayers, especially Mother Bachus and my brother Don, his great uncle.

Anita and I enjoy bringing Hazen to Memphis for week-long and summer visits. He is blessed to have close relationships with grandparents, great-grandparents, cousins, other relatives, St. Mark members, and dear friends of ours who treat him extra special. I began to teach him everything I knew. How to read the bible. How to catch and throw footballs and baseballs. How to dribble and shoot a basketball.

We would go places together - the gym, Benjamin L. Hooks Central Library, Tom Lee Park on the Mississippi River, Four-Way Restaurant, and Ms. Stein's Restaurant. Hazen and I would go to the movies together. I would get a nap while he watched the movie and enjoyed popcorn and Sprite. I fondly remember when two of my closest lifetime friends, Cornelius Yates and Brenda Hall, joined Hazen and me for lunch at Old Charley's restaurant when he was about eleven months old. For all of us, it was a celebration for the Mims family's first grandchild. Yates and Brenda were overjoyed with his presence and treated him like their grandchild. They played an integral part in the life of our children when they were growing up, along with another good friend, the late Chenata Jordan.

  Anita and I have been blessed to help raise Hazen like a son. Whereas both of us helped teach him how to read and play the card game Uno, I take sole credit for potty training him and teaching him how to tie his shoes. My good friend Pastor Jairus Winfrey taught Hazen and me how to fish during the coronavirus pandemic in 2020. Hazen, Anita, and I have also been road travelers, including taking a trip to California to visit Disneyland.

  We have been blessed to nurture Hazen with a servant spirit by allowing him to help deliver meals to Senior citizens on behalf of the Metropolitan Inter-Faith Association (MIFA). Hazen also lends a hand with St. Mark food donations and serving meals in the community. Anita and I have been blessed to help shape Hazen's personality to be a servant of God and a blessing to the community.

Before the Coronavirus pandemic, Anita and I would frequently host parties and invite people to the house. Anita was my guest list control manager, ensuring I didn't invite too many people. We hosted close friends we had known for years, family members, and church members who are longtime personal friends. There was an occasion when the kids were young when we had a party and sent them upstairs. This was grown folks' time to indulge in a little fun and relax from the stress of life and work. Mr. & Mrs. Richmond also hosted gatherings at their house, more than most, serving catfish, grilled chicken, spaghetti, coleslaw, and much more to the delight of saints and sinners, if there were any.

We would play the card game Spades, dance, eat delicious food, and have a good time. I always considered myself a pretty good Spades player back from my military days, when my military friends and I would play on Friday nights from sundown to sunrise. In later years, we connected with church members who introduced us to another card game, "Bid Whist," sometimes called "Bid Wiz." Deacon Sherman Johnson, Bro. Curtis Richmond, Deacon Preston Pittman, Rev. Alvin Casey, Sis. Georgia Torrance, and Sis. Mamie Richmond introduced us to the game. I found out that church friends are not only gifted spiritually but love to have fun and enjoy life outside the church… and were also card sharks!

Originating in London, the game of Bid Whist is now a tradition among African Americans.[27] Two of the hallmarks of the game are "rise and fly" (get up after you lose to make room for another team) and trash talking (bluffing, verbal jockeying). Bid whist was a difficult card game for me to master with the competition level I encountered. I tried playing with Anita but eventually had to join forces with a couple of male partners. The object of the game is to outsmart your opponent, even when your hand is bad. I later learned my greatest weakness was trying to control the bid with every hand, reflecting my tendency to manage and control things. I had to learn the strategy of the game, which meant learning how to trash talk to lead the other team to make a wrong move. I learned several psychological and strategic lessons playing with Deacon Johnson, Rev. Casey, Deacon Pittman, and Bro. Richmond. They had a way of rubbing in losing that taught me well. However, once I learned that in Bid Whist, it's not important to win the bid but to work with your partner to outsmart your opponent in playing each hand, I became a better player and enjoyed trash-talking

---

27   Greg Morrison and Yanick Rice Lamb. Rise and Fly: Tall Tales and Mostly True Rules of Bid Whist. Three Rivers Press, August 23, 2005. ISBN-10: 1400051681. https://www.npr.org/templates/story/story.php?storyId=5069913

right along with them! The joy and good times we shared are memories of a lifetime.

    Some of our other joyous memories are spending time visiting my parents in Greenville. Some Sundays, we would let my mother know we were coming, and she would have a spread of food on the table after church. She would fill her dinner table with fried chicken, greens, yams, potato salad, English peas, baked chicken breast, roast, turkey legs, dressing, macaroni and cheese, cabbage, and corn salad. Mom made delicious desserts like coconut cake, fruit salad, homemade ice cream, pound cake, and chocolate cake. It was like going to a soul food Restaurant with the option of getting everything on the menu. Mom was one of the best cooks in the world. I always went back for 2nd and 3rd helpings. However, there was one time we traveled as a family to Greenville to surprise her with a Sunday visit at church when things didn't turn out so well. When we arrived at New Mt. Zion, Mom was serving as an Usher as we entered the sanctuary. She was thrilled to see her grandchildren, Anita, and myself. Her love for family was demonstrated all over her face. After worship, we arrived at my parents' house expecting a feast, but there was no food prepared. This would be our family's last time giving my mom a surprise visit on a Sunday! I learned to announce our family plans to visit on Sundays ahead of time to give Mom plenty of time to prepare a delicious meal.

The Crossroads of Champions

When my hometown pastor, Rev. H. A. Armstrong, was approaching retirement, my mother felt I would be good for the church as a leader. She thought I could grow the church because I loved children, worked well with young males coaching baseball, and had a strong relationship with their parents. She'd witnessed the creation of BOLD Brothers and how I built a strong community of people organizing sports, leadership programs, and activities for families. I was reluctant to submit a resume to my home church because Memphis was three hours away, and I believe it requires more than preaching on Sunday to grow a church. I would need to be there during the week. I also knew about the dangers of Highway 61, a two-lane highway where fatal car crashes occur frequently. I reluctantly but wisely chose to stay in Memphis and focus on building our life there.

CHAPTER FIVE

Ministry Crossroads

The crossroads of my life and ministry unite in many ways with Rev. Dr. J. C. Bachus. I served in ministry under his leadership for 36 years. Our spiritual crossroads began in 1985 when he appointed me chairman of St. Mark's annual Men's Day and as a deacon. As a young deacon, I supported his ministry by attending numerous revivals and hearing him preach in many church gatherings throughout the city. I was introduced to many contemporary pastors and preachers of his generation. They had a strong bond with each other and fellowship among their churches.

In many traditional Black Baptist churches, deacons are limited to counting money or praying. However, in the bible, the position of deacon is not limited to devotional services or financial stewards; it's closely aligned with supporting the pastor, preaching, and teaching God's word. As such, I knew biblically it was my responsibility to support my Pastor and represent St. Mark to the best of my abilities. I treated my responsibilities as a Deacon with great importance because

I value commitment and faithfulness, character traits that have always meant a lot to me.

In 1989, I was the speaker for St. Mark's 2nd Sunday Men's Breakfast Fellowship. At the end of my presentation, I walked back to my seat, continuing to speak with zeal. Shortly after sharing the message that day, God called me to preach the gospel of Jesus Christ. Many people question how a person knows God is calling them to preach. The simplest way to explain my being called was there was a constant burning in my heart and spirit by the Holy Spirit about preaching the gospel of Christ. The idea of preaching was on my mind day and night. My commitment to bible study, prayer meetings, Sunday School, and Sunday night worship all contributed to my being called to preach. Deacon John W. Page, who also served as Superintendent of St. Mark's Sunday School, told me he was not surprised I was called to preach. I appreciated hearing that from Deacon Page, a highly respected deacon and strong leader of St. Mark.

I first shared my calling to preach with Anita and afterward informed Pastor Bachus. Neither of them was surprised. Pastor Bachus was calm, encouraging, and reassuring, and offered words of instruction. My mother, who had invested so much into me spiritually, was overjoyed to have her son become a preacher. My spiritual growth began with her love and taking me to church every Sunday.

I was 29 years old when I was called to preach, close to the age Jesus was when he began his earthly ministry. I found this to be symbolic of Jesus' ministry. I knew preaching was a high calling, as cited in ROMANS 10:15, *"How beautiful are the feet of them that preach the gospel of peace and bring glad tidings of good things!"* Pastor Bachus always held preaching foremost in his ministry. On some Sundays, he would preach during 11:00 a.m. worship, again at 3:00 p.m. during a visit to another church, and later that evening at 7:30 p.m. back at St. Mark. He exerted the same amount of energy in every sermon. Sometimes the night worship was more powerful and spiritual even with just a few folks in attendance. Pastor Bachus did not base his preaching on the size of the crowd. He preached to 2 or 3 people like it was 200 or 300.

One night I had to preach for a pastor in Memphis during a revival. It was so cold that snow and ice covered the ground, and I thought certainly the pastor would cancel the revival services. He did not. I called Anita to tell her the revival was still on for the night, and she showed up along with one member of the host church and the pastor. I preached like the house was full because that is what I saw in Pastor Bachus.

I knew preaching would require more biblical study and formal education. Pastor Bachus often spoke about his theological learning and how early in his ministry, he studied under the leadership of Rev. Dr. Herbert W. Brewster, one of the founders of the Tennessee School of Religion (TSOR), a local bible school in South Memphis.[28] This helped motivate me to enroll in TSOR, which at the time was led by Rev. Dr. Reuben Green. My teachers were Rev. Artis Golden, Rev. Ezekiel Bell, and some old-school preachers who taught the essentials of preaching. Rev. Golden had a familiar saying when it came to preaching, "Don't give people gospel indigestion." He cautioned young preachers like me to avoid trying to preach the whole Bible in one sitting. TSOR instructors taught us to read ourselves full, pray ourselves hot, and preach ourselves empty. They shared words of wisdom like, "The Lord does not call us for who we are but what we can be" and "Preachers need to be empowered with the Holy Ghost and preach within 15-25 minutes." This resonated with me because it seemed the average attention span during most sermons was about 25 minutes. We were also advised not to give the audience a replay of the news. "Tell them what Thus Saith the Lord."

Rev. Bell's familiar saying was, "Be yourself and don't try to imitate your pastor's preaching style." This was beneficial because

---

28   The Tennessee School of Religions, formerly known as J. L. Campbell School of Religion, and the Tennessee Baptist School of Religion, was founded in 1944 by a group of ministers namely, Reverends A.E. Campbell, L. R. Donson, A. H. Rice, A. J. Campbell, C. J. Gaston, C. H. Murphy, A. E. Freeman, A. L. Sadler, W. Herbert Brewster and James F. Estes, Esquire. From the History page of the "About Us" section of the Tennessee School of Religion website. https://tsormemphis.org/about/history/

when people are called to preach, they are exposed to many different preaching styles that can easily lead to imitating others. I never tried to preach like anyone else and did not practice preaching as some ministers do. I might have been better off if I did practice preaching! I learned through my study that the Holy Spirit is the true preacher, and the impact of preaching is determined by the Spirit of God. Pastor Bachus shared with me these words from his mentor Dr. Brewster: "There is something you can learn from any preacher, even if it is what not to do." TSOR provided a solid education for novice preachers in scripture and preaching and was a great springboard for pursuing more formal education in Theology.

My greatest reluctance to accept my call to preach was that I could not sing, and my critics let me know it. I recall somewhere in the late 90s, after a high and glorious Sunday worship celebration, being in Pastor Bachus' study and rubbing my hands on his shoulders, asking God for a double portion of his anointing. It was his anointing, prayer power, and gifted preaching style I desired and entreated the Lord for. Having been ridiculed by members for attempting to sing an Issac Watts hymn, I knew there was little hope of possessing Pastor Bachus' singing talent.

Dr. Watts' songs are a tradition in the black church. Unknown to most, Watts was an English Christian minister, hymn writer, and theologian considered the "Godfather of English Hymnody." The service at St. Mark often opened with one of his powerful hymns, which are congregational and led by an individual, followed by a repetitive response by members. Nobody at St. Mark sounded as good to me singing Dr. Watts hymns as Pastor Bachus and Anita. My favorite is "Father I Stretch My Hand to Thee." His hymns have a way of entering your spirit and causing God to anoint your prayer and preaching.

I witnessed many preachers who were gifted with the ability to sing. The masses in my circle expected preachers to sing and "hoop." To hoop means to preach with a particular cadence in your voice, a rhythmical style that black preachers love and many African-Americans churchgoers enjoy. I did not possess the gifts of singing or hooping. I am tone-deaf to music, so if there is any rhythm in my preaching, it is Holy Spirit-inspired. Ultimately, I did not allow my inability to sing or hoop to prevent me from accepting my call to preach the gospel. Preaching is about delivering the Word of God.

Many black Baptist preachers rejoice in a harmonic close. When it came to preaching, Pastor Bachus was a "Master Closer and Hooper." And he could also sing! Serving under a pastor with those gifts in a church where praise is key, those of us who didn't possess musical talent had to be comfortable with our spiritual gifts. God gave me the gift of illustration in my sermons and the ability to use visual aids in my preaching. I will often provide a demonstration during my sermon climax. Visual aids can be risky in preaching because there is always the potential for things to go wrong, but if they go as planned, it leaves a lasting impression.

Early in my ministry, I was always excited about Pastor Bachus' friends calling me to preach on Sunday morning. Many of my preaching opportunities were made possible because of his relationship with so many pastors. Pastor James Van Buren, Pastor R. S. Pamphlet, Pastor W. C. Ingram, Pastor William Henry Bass, Dr. C. P. Bounds, and many others extended me the privilege of declaring the word of God and developing my preaching ministry at their respective churches. Preaching on Sunday mornings at visiting churches was like being on television during prime time. I had supportive congregations and experienced the anointing of the Holy Spirit when I delivered God's word to His people. The fact that the congregations at visiting churches were often more responsive to my preaching than in my home church coincides with scripture: "A prophet is not without honor, but in his own country, and among his own kin, and in his own house." MARK 6:4-6.

Most of my preaching at St. Mark was limited to small crowds during night worship, but those experiences were essential to my development. Back then, St. Mark had evening bible study at 6:00 p.m. and night worship at 7:30 p.m. The night bible study was called Baptist Training Union (B.T.U.), where doctrinal teaching was emphasized regarding the Baptist denomination. During this time very few churches had night worship, but Pastor Bachus used this time to develop preachers at St. Mark. He would preach during night worship or assign an Associate Minister. His philosophy was to "use who showed up." Since Rev. Casey and I were faithful in attending B.T.U., we got to preach more often. There were numerous times near the conclusion of B.T.U. Pastor Bachus would say, "We're going over to the other side for night worship," and occasionally, "to hear a word from Rev. Mims."

I never overcame the anxiety that my name may be called on any given Sunday night, but Pastor Bachus had instructed us to study and always be ready. There were times you felt you did good and times you knew you "died," a preacher's term for not doing good! However, some members always made you feel like you did a great job. Rev. Casey's mother, Mother Rosie Mosby, who was also Pastor Bachus' sister, was one of those individuals. When other folks avoided me after I preached, she always had a smile and would say, "I enjoyed you, and you did good." Her kindness and warm words of encouragement were a welcome balm early in my ministry. She reminded me of my mother Peaches, always seeing the best in her son and never the failures.

I learned in preaching, that if you do good, people will flock to you. If you do bad, they will avoid you like a plague! And quite often, preachers are their own worst critics mentally, psychologically, emotionally, and spiritually. I remember preaching and giving the benediction at the end of a worship service at St. Mark in 2021, and the only person who came up to fellowship with me was a 7-year-old boy, Caddarik Tyshawn Simmons. Caddarik is full of life and a believer in Jesus. God often sends children to bless us when we are feeling downcast and disappointed. That day, Caddarik came to the altar and told me I had done a good job but I paid little attention to his remarks at that moment. It was when I was at home sitting down in my La-Z-Boy chair, relaxing and having a self-reflection (pity party) about the impact of my sermon, that the Lord reminded me of Caddarik's comments. God spoke to me and said, "I sent a child to encourage you; you missed the joy of him bringing you good news." Caddarik reminds me of my grandson Hazen; he is unafraid, loves to get in your face, and is excited about life! Caddarik saved me that day from spiritual depression!

Pastor Bachus often referenced in his preaching how, early in his ministry, when his son Rev. Rodney C. Bachus Sr. was only a child, he did something similar for him. Pastor Bachus had preached and was feeling discouraged afterward, and Rodney came to him and told him what a great job he had done. It's amazing how God can impact His people through children in worship and encouragement.

Pastor Bachus had his Associate Ministers preach during our spring and fall revivals. These times were extremely exciting for St. Mark's sons (preachers). As Associate Ministers, we didn't have an official role in the church, but the members supported us nonetheless in a mighty way with their attendance and giving.

My first Sunday morning sermon at St. Mark occurred when Pastor Bachus was out of town preaching. This was a rare occasion because he seldom missed Sunday morning worship at St. Mark. He always tried to make it back for Sunday worship if he was conducting a revival out of town. The people expected the Pastor to be at church on Sunday morning, and if they didn't see his Cadillac in his parking space, they cruised right on by. I had been preaching for a couple of years when I got the first opportunity to preach at 11 a.m. Sunday morning worship! Pastor Bachus had assigned Rev. Casey to lead worship and appointed me to preach, and it was a monumental and nervous time. It was such a glorious Sunday that the text and topic are still engraved in my mind 30 years later. The text was from GENESIS 1:1-3, and the topic was "God Said It." It was a short but exhilarating sermon. I experienced a power I had never felt before in my preaching. Back then, we recorded worship services on cassette tapes, and I got a copy of my Hall of Fame sermon. When Pastor Bachus returned, I knew he had listened to it and was pleased. When you do something major for the first time in church, it is engraved in your memory forever.

As soon as I began preaching, I sent my resume to numerous churches seeking to become a Pastor. I had a few interviews but was never called to Pastor a church. Often preachers feel the need to lead a church immediately after being called to preach. In hindsight, I was seeking to do something I wasn't yet qualified to do. I desired more opportunities to preach but didn't realize the responsibility and challenges that accompany leading a congregation. What we desire to do in life may not be God's plan or timing.

In 2003, I visited Progressive Baptist Church to hear Pastor Bachus preach in a revival. Progressive Baptist was located across the street from the Foote Homes housing projects. This was my introduction to Foote Homes and one of the greatest ministry opportunities of my lifetime. At the intersection of Danny Thomas and Mississippi Boulevards, Foote Homes opened in April 1940 as a segregated low-income public housing project in South Memphis. Thousands of black Memphians called it home.[29],[30] By 2003, the community was struggling with violent crime, drugs, and substandard housing, a downward spiral that contributed to it being demolished in 2017.

---

[29] Faber, Madeline. 2017. The last major vestige of segregation-era housing set for demolition. High Ground News. May 10, 2017. https://www.highgroundnews.com/features/FooteHomesHistory.aspx

[30] "Landmark and Legend." https://www.landmarkandlegend.com/foote-homes.html

After the revival, I noticed several young black males sitting in the church. I had been coaching baseball in Memphis for a long time and wanted to recruit more young black males into the sport, so I saw an opportunity to field a baseball team. The 15 players I recruited from Foote Homes became the St. Mark Church Baseball Team. Ministry meant more than simply preaching on Sundays. It meant connecting with the community so coaching them became a ministry for me, one of my first opportunities to minister beyond the walls.

Aramis Higgins, one of my Foote Homes recruits, was 14 years old when he started playing baseball for St. Mark. He was in the 8th grade and a leader on and off the field. We had a great player-coach relationship. He played the position of catcher, one of the most important positions on the field. A catcher has to be smart, alert, a motivator for his teammates, and a coach on the field. Aramis was that type of baseball player. After middle school, he attended Booker T. Washington (BTW) High School. He was in the 2011 graduating class when BTW won President Barack Obama's 2011 Race to the Top High School Commencement Challenge. The Commencement Challenge invited the nation's public high schools to submit applications demonstrating their commitment to preparing students for college and a career.[31]

---

31 Press Release. May 10, 2011. Booker T. Washington High School Wins Race to the Top Commencement Challenge. Office of the Press Secretary, The White House. https://obamawhitehouse.archives.gov/the-press-office/2011/05/10/booker-t-washington-high-school-wins-race-top-commencement-challenge

BTW won the competition after taking extraordinary steps to increase its graduation rate from 55% in 2007 to 81.6% in 2010, and create an environment where students like Aramis could excel.[32]

I was blessed to be at the Cook Convention Center when President Obama delivered BTW's 2011 commencement address. I did not have tickets to the event, but I dressed up in my Air Force blues uniform, decorated with my medals, ribbons, and stripes, and went to the Convention Center anyway. After the ticket holders started entering, I sat in the lower level with Ms. Ruby Wilson, the Soul Queen of Memphis, hoping for a chance to get in. I felt if anyone should be allowed in, it should be Ms. Wilson, an ambassador for Memphis. We had a nice conversation, and I was awed by her gracious personality. After waiting a while, Ms. Wilson and I were finally allowed access to the event. After passing through security, there we were in the midst of the grand celebration! This is another moment in life where God showed me how important it is to have determination. It was a joy to see a young man come from a tough environment and excel at one of Memphis' top schools, and a blessing to celebrate with Aramis and his mother.

☀

---

32 ""

Long before being appointed Pastor of St. Mark, I gained some experience as an Assistant Pastor at another church. In 2004, Rev. Dr. Neasbie Alston Sr., Pastor of Gospel Temple Baptist Church, contacted Pastor Bachus for a youth day preacher. Pastor Bachus sent me to Gospel Temple to preach for the occasion. Pastor Alston invited me back a couple more times to preach. After a few visits, he asked me to be his Assistant Pastor. We were sitting in the Pastor's study. I was very excited, to say the least. Rarely did black Baptist churches appoint Assistant Pastors to support the pastor in carrying out their official duties in leading the church. I couldn't accept the position without talking with Pastor Bachus. I'm sure Pastor Alston had already consulted with him about the matter. They were a special breed of Pastors who respected protocol and code of conduct among pastors. After Pastor Bachus gave his approval, it did not take me long to accept the offer. I don't remember praying much about it or even asking Pastor Alston about my responsibilities. I just knew it was an honor that would offer me the chance to serve God's people and preach more, and be a stepping stone to becoming a pastor. As a preacher, you always want to preach!

When I shared the news with my mother, she was overjoyed that Pastor Alston had selected me as his assistant pastor. On a few occasions, she traveled from Greenville to worship with us at Gospel Temple. Her joy radiated seeing me serve Pastor Alston and the Gospel Temple Church family; I was blessed to have her experience that with us.

On April 15, 2004, my mother had surgery for cervical cancer. We expected her to recover, but the following day, she died suddenly from complications from the surgery. Members of Gospel Temple and St. Mark showered us with love and support. Buses were chartered by both churches to attend her home-going celebration in Greenville, a beautiful service that was befitting for a woman who dedicated her life to serving God. My mother, Tereather Addie "Peaches" Russell Mims, was blessed with a wonderful, purposeful life and people who loved her dearly.

Before she passed, we traveled as a family on a 15-passenger van to Moreno Valley, California, to visit her brother Sylvester Russell Sr. We also traveled as a family to visit her brother Robert Russell Sr. in St. Louis. Then I invited her to travel with me to Atlanta, so I could purchase a car, and we could visit her Brother Jake Russell. She drove to Memphis from Greenville, and I drove her car to Atlanta. She spent the day visiting Uncle Jake while I was car shopping. She was blessed to visit all three of her brothers on these trips, unaware that this would be her goodbye. I realized later the impact of the trips and the precious time we spent together in her last days on earth. Although she died much earlier than we could have imagined, God orchestrated her life and allowed her to tell her family goodbye.

The opportunity to serve Pastor Alston and Gospel Temple was a blessing in terms of my spiritual growth and understanding of church dynamics. I learned about power struggles among church leadership, and the level of respect members have for their pastor. As Pastor Alston's Assistant Pastor, I engaged with the members and started visiting the elderly, sick, and shut-in. They were very grateful for these visits, and I also enjoyed them. I was available whenever Pastor Alston needed me - bible study, special church occasions, funerals, birthday celebrations, and many other events. During our first year at Gospel Temple, Anita alternated Sundays, attending St. Mark and Gospel Temple. As we grew to love the members of Gospel Temple and they grew to love and accept us, Anita committed to attending every Sunday. After a year, she got involved with children and the Youth Choir and did a fantastic job working with them.

After two years, Pastor Alston assigned me to teach his early Sunday morning bible class. I was slightly timid because I had plenty of experience preaching but very little leading a bible study group. However, I grew and learned to prepare my lessons in advance and structure them based on a three-point outline form. There were numerous educators in the congregation at Gospel Temple, some of who pursued the truth by cross-referencing scripture after scripture. The words of Pastor Alston always echoed in my ear, "You learn by doing."

This was his way of saying I would grow by doing. Only a few attended early morning bible study, but they appreciated my three-point outline teaching style, perhaps because some were educators themselves! One member graciously gave me a note saying how my 3-point teaching style and preaching helped her immensely. Teaching bible study, you have to be prepared to answer questions from people who have more bible knowledge than you. You have to be aware of people who try to test your bible knowledge, something Jesus experienced with teachers of the law. You also have to avoid people who try to get you to "chase rabbits," a term for people who lead you down a path of discussion that has nothing to do with the lesson. Often the person is intentional in doing it. For me, preparation is essential, and relying on the Holy Spirit to lead and guide me in teaching and staying on track.

Gospel Temple inspired me to enroll at the Memphis Center for Theological Studies (MCUTS) for formal study in theology. MCUTS recruited mainly African-American preachers and Christian leaders, primarily male with some females from different denominations. As students, we had great teachers and a close-knit fellowship among one another. I was growing in the word of God, theological understanding of the scriptures, and hermeneutical study of the bible. MCUTS provided a path to obtaining an accredited bachelor's degree from Crichton College, a private for-profit nondenominational Christian College founded as Mid-South Bible Center in 1944. I completed my studies at MCUTS in 18 months and transferred to Crichton College, which accepted all my credits from MCUTS. At the time of my enrollment, Crichton was accredited by the Southern Association of Colleges and Schools and offered a range of majors, including Biblical Studies, teacher education, music, and others. I was part of a more diverse group of students there. The staff was very professional, and our professors challenged us to embrace Crichton's motto: "Think critically, grow spiritually, and change the world."[33]

The courses challenged me as never before, requiring extensive research and detailed writing. I delayed taking math courses until I finished all my other studies. Years earlier, I had struggled with algebra at the University of Memphis and had to drop out of the class, mainly because I struggled to understand my teacher's English. At Crichton, I was fortunate to have a brilliant math teacher, Mrs. Yanli Cui, who offered extra tutoring after class. I took advantage of extra tutoring from Mrs. Cui and the help I received from a friend in class. Anita enrolled at Crichton shortly after me. She studied at night, while I mostly had day classes, but we were blessed to graduate together in 2007. She earned a bachelor's degree in Organizational Management, and I earned a bachelor's degree in Biblical Studies.

---

[33] Later on, Crichton college was renamed Victory University. The school closed in 2014.

A young lady named Barbara Pruitt was in one of my few remaining classes at Crichton. She was in another course I'd taken, but we did not develop a friendship until that last class, where we sat next to each other. I enjoyed my classes more when I struck up friendships with other students, especially the one who helped me pass math! One day Ms. Pruitt gave me a note that read, "My church is going to South Africa next year. Would you like to go?" It was one of my great hopes to one day travel to Africa and visit the Motherland. I returned the note, asking her to check with her pastor to see if it was okay. She wrote back, "You are talking to the person who can make it happen!" As the Administrative Assistant at New Direction Christian Church, she had a role in planning and organizing the trip.

I realized then the great favor I had with God and my classmate! God was granting my desire to travel to Africa. I didn't know much about the trip, but I knew almost immediately I was going. After class, I came home and told Anita I was going to South Africa. Unfortunately, I did not ask her to travel with me. It wasn't just that the trip cost almost $3,000 per person. Our finances were more stretched back then, but we could have made it happen. The reality is that it was something I wanted to do for myself. As a married man, it was wrong for me to not take into consideration how Anita felt about all of it - my being asked by someone she didn't know to travel with a church she wasn't familiar with to a foreign country, and my having this great desire to experience a once in a lifetime trip on my own. Years later, therapy would help me examine the "man in the mirror" and gain a deep appreciation for the gem I have in Anita.

I was blessed with Ms. Pruitt's kind offer and the opportunity to visit the Motherland with New Direction Christian Church and their Pastor, Dr. Stacy Spencer. The mission trip was designed to provide medical and dental treatment for people living in Idutywa (now known as Dutywa), a town in the Eastern Cape province of South Africa. Idutywa was a rural area with poor infrastructure – no hospital, dirt roads, and an inadequate water system.

I desired to travel to Africa for many years, probably because of my strong and spiritual connection with my elders and roots. That connection was strengthened in 1977 when, like millions of Americans, I sat in front of the televisions for days mesmerized by Alex Haley's mini-series *Roots*. *Roots* was partly based on the Haley Family's transatlantic journey from the Gambia region of West Africa to Henning, Tennessee. *Roots* captured my attention as a teenager because I'd grown up with myths and lies about Africa, that it was an inferior place of uncivilized black people living in jungles. *Roots* showed how Africans were kidnapped from loving and stable families and communities and sold into slavery. It showed the horrors of crossing the Atlantic under inhumane conditions, and the hardships slaves endured after they arrived in America. *Roots* also showed America another story, the story of our humanity and resilience in earning our freedom. I was anxious to visit Africa and connect with people from the cradle of civilization whose DNA helped us survive all of it.

I started preparing for the trip in March 2007. I quickly applied for a passport and attended a planning meeting with the church, where I met Charlesetta Gipson, the travel agent who coordinated our trip. She shared the itinerary, advised us on what to pack, and instructed us on the customs of South Africans. Before the trip, I exchanged U.S. dollars for RAND, the South African currency, so I'd have plenty of spending money. This was a trip of a lifetime, so I invested in a new cellphone that would take great pictures. I also purchased a new adapter to work with electrical outlets in South Africa.

New Direction had a church in South Africa. A spiritual friend of Dr. Spencer's led the church and helped to assign preachers in our entourage to preaching opportunities there. Having a chance to preach the gospel in South Africa made it even more exciting for me. New Direction had shipped supplies and medical equipment in advance to fulfill the part of the mission dedicated to providing dental treatment and minor medical assistance. During our mission trip, while the medical staff was providing services inside a building, I spent time outdoors in the heat praying and interceding for men and women in Idutywa. I initiated an unannounced prayer meeting outdoors, and only a few people came forward. It was around noon when this occurred. The line grew longer and longer as more people desired intercessory prayer. It was a different feeling spiritually than being in America, where people are hesitant to embrace public prayer that isn't part of their tradition. In Idutywa, people were receptive to the invitation, waiting patiently in the heat of the day. After 90 minutes of praying for people, I was spiritually and physically drained and sweating all over my body. Several New Direction team members pulled me inside, sat me down, and prayed for my strength to be restored.

We spent our first few days doing mission work and the last three days touring the area. We visited several villages and the cities of Johannesburg and Soweto and many sites, including the Hector Pieterson Museum, named after the 12-year-old Black South African who was shot and killed by police during the 1976 Soweto uprising. The iconic image of Pieterson's body being carried away had the same effect on ending apartheid that pictures of Emmitt Till's mutilated body had on the civil rights movement in the U.S. Those images stripped away the pretense, mobilizing people around the globe to act. We also visited the Lesedi Cultural Village, Nelson Mandela's home, his birthplace in Mvezo, and enjoyed Africa's natural beauty during a wildlife safari.

Everywhere I went, I witnessed great love, unity, joy, and pride among South African people. The trip was a wonderful experience.

The South Africa mission trip was an eye-opener for me. Our mission work focused on providing aid to people who lived in settlements and shanty towns. Most of them lived in shacks made from tin or other materials that could be assembled in a few hours. These settlements lacked adequate sanitation, water, electricity, and sewage. They didn't have the necessities I enjoyed daily, such as fresh running water. Even so, my experience there taught me a lot about resilience. They had joy and a love for life that transcended their physical circumstances. It reminded me of my grandparents' lives on the farm. I always thought my grandparents were poor. They had automobiles, but they didn't have an indoor restroom. Both of my parents grew up using an outhouse. Growing up, I recall visiting churches in rural Mississippi that also didn't have running water or indoor restrooms. I remember how the Holy Spirit would fill those churches! I later realized that my grandparents were more joyful than many people I knew who lived in the city. Many of the South Africans I met seemed joyful in that same way.

Of course, not all black South Africans are poor, nor is the nation stagnant in making progress. On the contrary, South Africa's economy is diverse and growing, and the country is the most technologically advanced nation in Africa. Black freedom fighters and human rights activists won one of the most significant battles of the 20th century by garnering international support to end apartheid, the political system that legalized racial oppression of non-white South Africans. Although poverty and unemployment remain high, South Africa has progressed since apartheid was officially dismantled. It took a Civil War to end slavery in the U.S. South Africa ended apartheid without a coup.

The mission trip to South Africa showed me how important it was to perform ministry outside the four walls. When I returned home, I knew God had a new assignment for me, and I had a heart for the community to evangelize and reach the unsaved for Christ.

It was also about this time I felt the Holy Spirit leading me to leave Gospel Temple. To a certain degree, I felt trapped as the Assistant Pastor because I wasn't able to accomplish what the Holy Spirit was calling me to do. I couldn't implement the vision God gave me to have a greater impact on the community that was first ignited by ministering to a baseball team from Foote Homes. Preaching and doing mission work in South Africa felt like wind blowing on that flame. It changed my mind about material things and evangelism. I had to break away from the traditional church focus, which too often is directed towards the internal functions of the church while devoting little attention to ministering to people in need outside of those walls.

I knew in my heart that I wanted to reach people in the community, and I needed the freedom to do God's will as a Pastor. When I told Pastor Alston I was leaving Gospel Temple, he asked me, "How long have you been with me?" I told him three years. He said, "It went by so fast that you owe me another three years!" Pastor Alston and I enjoyed a father-and-son relationship. He trusted me with the members of the church and often shared his wisdom to prepare me for being a Pastor someday. Anita and I attended annual birthday and Christmas celebrations hosted by Pastor Alston and his wife, Dr. Bettye Alston, at their beautiful home. His wife always complimented me on how well I cared for Pastor Alston, and appreciated my concern for him. During my last several months serving Pastor Alston, I became his church chauffeur picking him up in my red 1994 Lexus ES 300. The car was emblematic of him, and he enjoyed the ride. He was a smooth and cool gentleman and fancy dresser. I was honored to provide the care and love.

Pastor Alston had been a pastor for over 40 years. "You have to answer the call of God upon your life," he told me upon my departure. On our last Sunday at Gospel Temple, he had the church raise a love offering for us. They thanked us for our service and showered us with love and gifts. Although many were sad to see me go, I felt a few in the crowd were happy. The church's strong governing official staff conflicted with my view of pastoral leadership. My nontraditional approach to worship and preaching did not always align with their expectations and norms. On one occasion, when Pastor Alston was away, I introduced fellowshipping among the members during worship. Pastor Bachus did this occasionally during worship to get members to express love for one another. When the news got back to Pastor Alston, he called and told me one of the deacons was in opposition to this. He politely forbade me to engage in future activities like that. I was shocked because I was accustomed to the Pastor setting the tone and directing the flow of worship as led by the Holy Spirit. I drafted a resignation letter and gave it to him the following Sunday. After reading it, he told me, "If you run, you will always be running." I didn't see it as running but being restricted in leading God's people in worship. However, I realized Pastor Alston was correct and rescinded my letter of resignation.

    I often shared whatever difficulties I encountered at Gospel Temple with Pastor Bachus, and he would give me words of wisdom to help me stay committed to serving Pastor Alston. In hindsight, it was a great act of unselfishness for Pastor Bachus to release Anita and me to lend our time, talent, and finances to support another church. Blessing me to serve Pastor Alston and Gospel Temple also renewed a historical connection between the two churches. A news clipping on the wall outside of Pastor Alston's study featured the two churches fellowshipping together in the early 1900s, the period when both of them were founded. During this period, St. Mark's founding pastor, Rev. B. J. Wilson, and one of the pastors of Gospel Temple often worshiped together.

Pastor Bachus always encouraged ministers to walk by faith, follow their dreams and pursue opportunities to minister and preach. He never tried to hold them back from starting ministries or following the direction of the Holy Spirit, another reason why he allowed me to serve under Pastor Alston. When I informed Pastor Bachus that I was resigning from Gospel Temple, I also shared my plan to start a ministry. He gave me his blessings and wished Anita and me well. I often heard him say, "If you can make a difference in the life of one person, you have made a difference." Those inspiring words constantly refreshed my commitment to ministry.

In 2007, I launched Land on the Rock Ministry, a ministry we later defined as a church. The name came from the scripture MATT. 16:18, where Jesus tells Peter based on his confession, "and on this rock I will build my church..." The symbolic meaning behind the name was we can safely land on Jesus when we are in trouble. We started the ministry with just a few of us, my close friend Bro. Tyrone Taylor, my cousin Kent Bruno Russell, our daughter Tracy Ann, longtime friends Joy Brassfield and Shazia Brassfield, and Bro. Steven Snipes, who served with me in the Air Force. Bro. Snipes was our organist as well. Paula Taylor, another longtime friend who lived in the neighborhood, supported our bible study. Later God would give us an additional sainted soul, Ms. LaDonna Horne, who became like a mother to me as well as a spiritual encourager. There would be occasional visits from other friends and family.

We started small, but with great expectations that we would grow, at least that was my expectation. Unlike most of Memphis, there was not an abundance of black churches in the Raleigh area where we lived. I had the vision to unite people in Raleigh and impact the community with the word of God and worship. I truly believed I was on my way to growing a large congregation.

We had opening day worship on New Year's Day of 2007, with friends and family present to support us. Our members canvassed the neighborhoods inviting people to church, trying to reach the unchurched and unsaved. We went door to door, sharing our faith and distributing flyers with our worship schedule. It was exciting for our members because we were fulfilling the Great Commission found in MATT. 28:19, where Jesus commissioned the disciples to *"Go ye therefore, and teach all nations, baptizing them in the name of the*

Father, and of the Son, and the Holy Ghost." It was exciting for me to see young adults carrying out the Great Commission and supporting my God-given vision. We used the BOLD Brothers van to transport youth from Foote Homes to minister to them and have them be a part of worshipping God.

Things did not go as I had planned. I wanted to grow a church full of adults. God was having us impact the lives of many youths, but I got frustrated because our church did not attract adult members. Only one lady from the neighborhood joined our church; it wasn't long before we lost her. It takes time to grow a church. People are attracted to crowds, so growing a small church is difficult. I looked for reasons why our ministry wasn't growing and blamed it on "location, location, location," a phrase common in business and applicable to churches. At our first location, we rented a chapel from a ministry for people who lived alternative lifestyles that weren't in line with Christian biblical teaching. They had been an item of controversy in the local news. That ministry operated in the facility Monday through Friday. Land on the Rock rented the chapel for our Sunday worship. I believe people associated the building with the controversy, which hindered our growth. It probably didn't help to start a church in a city known for having a church on every corner. Memphis ranks 5th in the nation in terms of churches per capita.

Our second location was on the outskirts of Memphis in the town of Bartlett, Tennessee. We leased a church building and had to opt for a 6:00 p.m. worship time because it was the only time slot available. Strategically, it wasn't a good location or an ideal time for a worship service.

Our third location was our home. We had more attendees there than at any other location. One summer, we offered a full week of Vacation Bible School (VBS) at our home and had volunteers help us. One of our longtime neighbors, Mrs. Lisa Dillard, volunteered to assist with VBS and did an excellent job teaching young ladies.

To witness Anita transform our home into a church was a blessing from God. She sectioned certain rooms in our house for children based on ages and sex to accommodate VBS. The level of love and support she demonstrated to children and the people of God was incredible. I admired her for allowing me to open our home to strangers and helping me live my dream of reaching people, which also became her mission.

Our church ministry expanded to residents of Foote Homes. When we formed Land on the Rock Ministry, we asked parents in the Foote Homes community if their children could come to our ministry, and many consented. Several baseball players' siblings, including their sisters, attended our worship. This gave Anita and other women from our ministry the opportunity to mentor them. Many children living in

Foote Homes weren't exposed to the traditional two-parent household Anita and I grew up in. I had to explain to some of them why, as a married couple, the two of us lived together in the same house. Some thought we were rich because we lived in a large house in the suburbs. This helped me understand how growing up in poverty shapes a child's perception of what is normal. Child poverty creates gaps in cognitive skills for young children, jeopardizes their health and ability to learn, and fuels an intergenerational cycle of poverty (Children's Defense Fund, 2022).[34] It gave us unspeakable joy to help them see a world beyond Foote Homes. Many factors influence a child's life, and many children who grew up in Foote Homes became adults who lead fulfilling and productive lives.

On Wednesdays, we hosted bible study on the playground at Foote Homes. On one occasion, I was ill and couldn't attend bible study. Anita, my cousins Gretchen and Calvin Graham, Joy Brassfield, and Shazia Brassfield carried out the work of the ministry. When Anita got home, she brought me good news of their great time teaching the children God's word. A young girl about 7 years old asked her, "Where's the God-man?" This comment highlighted our impact on children in the most impoverished area of Memphis. God allowed us to transform a playground into a bible study ground, play area, outdoor dance floor,

---

[34] Policy Priorities: Child Poverty. Children's Defense Fund, 2022. https://www.childrensdefense.org/policy/policy-priorities/child-poverty/

block party venue, and so much more for families in Foote Homes to enjoy. Our grandson Hazen was about 3 years old at that time. He comes from a middle-class family, but kids will be kids. They don't choose playmates based on income levels. He enjoyed his playmates at Foote Homes because they were a kid like him.

Through our ministry in Foote Homes, God transformed our minds about the impact we were having on families. It was a blessing to have BOLD Brothers and St. Mark partner with us for three years. Our partnership was uplifted by faithful service and support from Anita, Shazia Brassfield, Joy Brassfield, Renee Brassfield, Gretchen Russell, Calvin Russell, Tyrone Taylor, Patrick Bachus, Timothy Bachus, and Suzette Twilley. Our challenges were not a deterrent to our mission to spread the gospel, give hope, share joy, and make a difference in people's lives.

Although we had a lot of success reaching youth, Land on the Rock did not attract adult members. In three years, we had moved from one worship location to another church building, then to our home. We had lost most of our adult support for reasons unknown. I began to question whether it was the locations, my preaching, or that Memphis had enough churches already. Because we were not growing numerically as a church, I began to suffer depression and almost dreaded Sundays.

A passage of scripture that spoke to me is ST. MARK 11:12-20, where Jesus curses an unproductive fig tree. The spiritual connotation is the tree represents Jews who rejected Jesus. When Jesus cursed the fig tree, his disciples heard it. The following day they passed by the fig tree, and the disciples were shocked the tree was dried up from the roots. I had given the church three years to grow. My heart was burdened with having to transition to another phase in ministry. Instead of attempting to make something grow that wasn't growing, it was time to accept reality: I didn't have to do something that did not bring me joy. Just as God had led me to start the ministry, I believe He led me to discontinue it. My time with Land on the Rock taught me a lot, mostly never to be too afraid of change and to walk by faith. It also helped to humble me because I had never failed at anything before, and it felt like a failure.

When I decided to end the ministry, I no longer felt stuck and depressed. Anita always had confidence in my being led by the Lord and agreed with my decision. Throughout everything, she was always there. Rev. Ronald Hampton asked me if I had ceased preaching. Rev. Hampton is Pastor of Right Directions Christian Ministry and one of my closest friends. I was closing the ministry, but I had not finished preaching.

The final closure came when we no longer placed a large sign with my picture in front of our house on Sundays inviting people to worship. The sign was moved to the backyard; I still have it, a reminder of my trials, tribulations, and triumphs during that journey. Initially, closing the ministry seemed like a failure, but I found solace leaning on Pastor Bachus' words, "If you can make a difference in the life of one person, you have made a difference." I knew that we had made a difference in many lives. In recent years, several young black males who worshiped with Land on the Rock Ministry in our home fifteen years ago rang our doorbell to let us know they were grateful for the seeds we sowed in their lives.

Legendary NFL Coach Bill Walsh said," Many people erroneously think they only have one chance to succeed in their life's work, and if they miss that chance, they are doomed to failure. In fact, most people have several opportunities to succeed." Coach Walsh was not allowed the opportunity to be the head coach of the Cincinnati Bengals when their legendary Coach Paul Brown retired. Walsh would later become the Head Coach of the San Francisco 49ers and defeat the Cincinnati Bengals in the Superbowl. Most of us will have several opportunities to succeed.

Pastor Bachus was a constant source of encouragement for me though my experiences with Gospel Temple and Land on the Rock. When I shared my troubles and sought his advice, it was encouraging to hear him, "You can always come home." When we went home to

St. Mark, I was relieved and no longer stressed from trying to make the ministry I started work. Anita and I got a loving reception from our St. Mark family! There's something powerful about knowing that regardless of where life leads us, there's a place where we can land safely. It made our landing even more special when Land on the Rock's sainted soul, Ms. LaDonna Horne, not only embraced us returning to St. Mark; she became part of our family there! In July 2021, Anita and I visited a member of St. Mark, Sis. Magdalene Mathis, at her home. She told us that halting our ministry was God's way of bringing us back home. I can honestly say after traveling down a road of frustration, disappointments, failures, and depression, God led us to victory!

CHAPTER SIX

Rev. Dr. Johnny Clarence ("J.C.") Bachus "Cowboy"

Witnessing Rev. Dr. Johnny Clarence ("J. C.") Bachus' greatness as a pastor and leader, his love for family, and his humility for over forty years inspired me to write a book to share his life with others for years to come. I started documenting his journey in 2014. He was humbled by the thought of me creating a historical account of his life and ministry. On numerous occasions, I met with him privately in his pastor's study to discuss his ministry and life. We also had many conversations at his residence, surrounded by his family. He was deeply loved by his family, some of whose thoughts about him are also included in this chapter. For most of this chapter, I'll call him Pastor Bachus.

Pastor Bachus was a living legend who was highly respected by his peers in ministry, both contemporary preachers and novice ministers. He was given the nickname "Cowboy" by his longtime friend, the late Rev. Dr. James Adams. It was only befitting for his wardrobe to include cowboy boots and cowboy hats that complimented each other. He was a modern-day cowboy who came to the rescue of those oppressed. That nickname caught on, and it amused him to hear it at the National Baptist Convention meetings and other places. I enjoyed the stories told by Pastor Bachus' longtime friends in the ministry who journeyed with him on the path from his early years to his rise to national recognition.

***

Johnny Clarence Bachus was born on December 16, 1935, in Hernando, Mississippi, a small town in the northwest corner of the state about 25 miles south of Memphis. His parents, Eddie Bachus Sr. and Leona Bachus, were born and raised in Mississippi. They owned the home and farm in Hernando, where they raised a large family with 14 children. At times grandchildren lived there as well. Johnny was their ninth child and fifth son. Mr. Bachus served as a deacon at Rising Sun Missionary Baptist Church in Hernando, led by Rev. N. A. Crawford. The entire family attended Rising Sun, where Johnny accepted Christ when he was 11.

Johnny Bachus graduated valedictorian from his high school, Baptist Industrial (B.I.) College in Hernando, Mississippi. Founded in 1900 by the North Mississippi Baptist Educational Convention, B.I. was the first school in DeSoto County to offer African Americans instruction through grade twelve and one of the earliest private schools for African Americans in north Mississippi.[35] The school closed in 1960. I remember one of Pastor Bachus' friends jokingly saying there were only 5 people in the graduating class. I have no idea how many people graduated with him, but I don't ever recall anyone questioning how smart he was.

In the fall of 1955, Johnny moved to Memphis, residing with his older sister Bessie Lou and her husband, Floyd Millon. He attended LeMoyne-Owen College and enjoyed singing in a choir and a quartet with his brothers. Memphis was only 25 miles away from Hernando, so Johnny traveled back to Mississippi frequently, singing at church functions with the quartet. That's how he met the love of his life, John Ella Johnson. The quartet was performing at a musical at Halliburton Baptist Church in Nesbit, Mississippi. John Ella was there singing with the choir from her church, Bethlehem Missionary Baptist Church. She made eye contact with Johnny, unforgettable glances as she remembered them. She had seen him before at various church concerts and asked her cousin John Luster about him. John introduced them in the summer of 1956, and they began courting a year later.

Dating involved picking her up at her parents' house and going to his mom's house in Hernando, where they would spend the entire day together. They often went to church together, to the movies, out to

---

[35] Baptist Industrial College Marker, visitmississipp.org, https://www.mississippimarkers.com/desoto-county.html

eat, and sometimes to her parents' house. The Gay Hawk restaurant in Memphis was one of their favorite places. One of the things John Ella loved about him was he made her laugh a lot by telling funny jokes, especially when he was around family members.

Johnny married his sweetheart John Ella on her birthday, January 2, 1958. As newlyweds, they lived in Memphis with Bessie Lou, Floyd, and their six children. For John Ella, living with Bessie Lou was like living with close family. Floyd had a garden in the backyard where they gathered vegetables to cook.[36] Bessie Lou enjoyed cooking for her family, and John Ella helped with cooking and taking care of the children.

Eventually, Johnny and John Ella moved to the Walker Homes subdivision in South Memphis, where they raised their children. Walker Homes was financed and built by Dr. Joseph Edison Walker, founder of the Universal Life Insurance Company and one of the most prominent African Americans in the U.S. He also hailed from the Mississippi. Like my great grandfather, James Henry Russell Sr., Dr. Walker was influenced by the ideas of forward-thinking Black people who lived in the Mississippi Delta and promoted economic self-sufficiency.

---

[36] A personal reflection on her husband, Rev. Dr. J.C. Bachus, John Ella Bachus, 2021

Rev. Dr. Johnny Clarence ("J.C.") Bachus

Johnny Bachus was called to preach the gospel of Jesus Christ on January 1, 1966. He told his brother, Pastor C.L. (Clemmie) Bachus, that God had called him to preach, then he told John Ella. His brother had previously announced his calling in 1963. Rev. Johnny Clarence ("J.C.") Bachus preached his first sermon at Rising Sun Missionary Baptist Church in Hernando, Mississippi, his home church growing up. His parents had passed, Eddie in 1958 and Leona in 1964, but John Ella was there with some of his siblings.

His good friend, the late Rev. John Lee (J.L.) Payne, knew that the pastor of St. Mark Missionary Baptist Church in Memphis had passed after serving for only one year, and the church was looking for a new pastor. The search committee was spearheaded by Deacon John W. Page and Sis. Rosie Ella Gray, Church Secretary. They didn't want just a good preacher. They were searching for a good pastor and leader. Rev. Payne recommended his friend Rev. J. C. Bachus.

Rev. Benjamin J. Wilson organized St. Mark Missionary Baptist Church (MBC) along with ten loyal members in 1910. After occupying space on Main Street Extended and later Wallace Place at Long Street, the congregation purchased a permanent location at 940 South Lauderdale Street. The small imitation brick structure cost $2300, which the congregation paid in installments.

Rev. Wilson was not only the pastor and a teacher of God's word; he was a visionary who focused his ministry toward "a Greater St. Mark." When the structure on South Lauderdale Street was renovated in 1959, the name on the cornerstone was changed to "The Greater St. Mark Baptist Church." The name didn't catch on, which is why it's still called St. Mark Missionary Baptist Church today.

When Rev. Wilson organized the church, he was employed as a coal peddler. Even after he became pastor, he continued working for several years. During Rev. Wilson's ministry, he worked Monday through Saturday, and served as the deacon and janitor. On Sundays, he taught and preached God's word. Rev. Wilson was well known throughout the city and surrounding areas, and the church grew under his leadership. He served faithfully for 55 years, and when he passed in the spring of 1965, he'd been a minister longer than any other pastor of a Black church in Memphis. He was succeeded by Rev. Woodrow W. Miller, who was elected pastor in May 1965 and served faithfully until he passed in May 1966.

At the invitation of the search committee, Rev. J. C. Bachus preached his first sermon at St. Mark MBC in August of 1966. In October of that year, he was elected the third Pastor of St. Mark. One of the other candidates was Rev. Joseph McGhee. Deacon Preston Pittman, a lifelong faithful member, recalled what happened when Rev. Bachus learned that he was elected: "The evening that he left the home of my grandmother, Mrs. Rosie Gray, who was secretary of St. Mark, he had been informed that he had been elected the Pastor of St. Mark Baptist Church. A proud, humble, and confident man walked out of that house. The next Sunday, he walked into St. Mark, not knowing what to expect but maintaining a confident demeanor about himself. Based on my lifetime membership at St. Mark, I can truly say that Pastor Bachus 'walked by faith and not by sight,' 2 CORINTHIANS 5:7, always leading by example."[37]

Pastor Bachus preached his first sermon as pastor of the fifty-six-year-old St. Mark MBC on Sunday, November 6, 1966. At the time, the church had a small flock of only thirty congregants, mostly senior citizens, including a few founding members. One of the ways he would grow the church would be by getting more young people involved. People were attracted to the fact he made them feel important and special in the eyesight of God. His preaching and teaching were truthful, motivational, inspirational, and based on sound biblical doctrine. He methodically made decisions to prevent himself from showing favoritism to members of the congregation, especially his family. This also helped the church to grow spiritually and numerically.

---

[37] Personal Reflection, Deacon Preston Pittman, St. Mark Missionary Baptist Church, Memphis, TN, 2021

When he was first elected pastor, the average weekly offering was $30. On one particular Sunday, Pastor Bachus contributed $18 of the aggregate amount. He knew the success or failure of the church was on his shoulders as the leader, so he gave extra when the membership was small. Pastor Bachus was not a tither initially. During our many conversations, he acknowledged he pastored for some time before committing to tithing and confessed it is a growth area for Saints. He told me the church spent all day one Saturday selling hot dogs and only had a small profit to show for it after expenses. This led him to focus on teaching about giving to God based on biblical principles. He was a liberal giver to the Lord but conservative in other areas of his life.

Pastor Bachus taught bible studies on Wednesday nights, preached the gospel on Sundays, and worked a secular job like his predecessors. He worked five days a week as a factory laborer with International Harvester to support his growing family. The International Harvester plant in Memphis manufactured agricultural equipment. He was the family's sole provider until 1988, when Mother Bachus entered the field of employment. To keep costs down at St. Mark, he made repairs himself and served as the janitor, ensuring the church stayed clean just like Rev. Wilson had done.

Of course, I didn't know Pastor Bachus during those years of struggle, so hearing him talk about it was a privilege, especially the times that inspired him to walk by faith. Early in his ministry, during a revival he attended, he pulled out a $20 bill and a $1 bill during the offering. He placed the $20 bill in the offering. He was reluctant to give all he had, but it proved to be a test of faith in whether God would provide. After the worship service Rev. Jasper Williams, Sr. blessed him with $10, not knowing that Pastor Bachus had given his all in the offering. This was one of many signs early in his ministry that if he was obedient and walked by faith, God would supply his needs. Pastor Bachus worked for International Harvester for eleven years before resigning to pursue ministry full-time. When he came home and told his family he had quit his job, his oldest son Patrick was shocked and wondered out loud how the family was going to survive financially. Pastor Bachus was momentarily rocked by this question from his young son, who was only a teenager. He reassured his family God would provide.

Walking by faith did not mean Pastor Bachus would not get fearful on the journey. Shortly after leaving International Harvester, he was at the church one day when the phone rang. He had just had the phone installed at the church. He answered and heard, "This is McKinnon from Oak Ridge, Rev. Bachus. Can you come up here and do a revival for me? I'll take care of you." Pastor Dozier McKinnon from True Light Missionary Baptist Church in Oak Ridge, Tennessee, gave him his first revival opportunity after he left International Harvester.

Pastor Bachus said at that time, he didn't have money anywhere or anywhere to preach other than St. Mark. "I was fearful because I had been at my job eleven years, and it was the best paying job I ever had." That was the start of a remarkable relationship between Pastor Bachus and True Light MBC. He'd carry on a revival there for 35 consecutive years, 26 years for Pastor Dozier and 9 more years for Pastor Darris Waters. His last year at True Light MBC was 2010.

Herman Bachus remembers his older brother being frugal throughout his life. "Pastor Bachus was always going to hold on to a dollar, always, and everybody ended up borrowing money from him, even his brothers." Herman recalled how Pastor Bachus and others would work in the fields to have a little money. While Pastor Bachus held on to his, the others would spend theirs and then have to go to him. "They called him Skemy," Herman said. "If you borrowed money from him, you had to always come back with something in return."

Herman didn't grow up with his siblings because they were much older than him, but as an adult, he lived near Pastor Bachus in Memphis on Yokley Cove. Pastor Bachus was an inspiration who gave him solid advice. "Remember, there might come a rainy day and you will need something," Pastor Bachus told him. "Don't just get rid of everything you got." According to Herman, Pastor Bachus grew up with that mindset, and it defined who he was as a Pastor, "conservative yet always positioned to be a blessing to others, and strategically having the church in a position to be a blessing to others financially."[38]

Anita gave wonderful examples of her father's frugal nature. "My dad purchased the groceries. We didn't know what fast food meant! Mom was an amazing cook. Breakfast, lunch, and dinner, all at home." Anita recalled how when Patrick, Rodney, and herself turned 16, their father took them to a job that he had previously scoped out and selected for them to work. They had to save to purchase their senior ring, invitations, etc. "Do your job," he'd say. According to Anita, "He was not wasteful with money. Period! If there was a need, it was provided. No name brand clothing, but we had quality provisions." God did provide.

As it was throughout the U.S., the 1960s were a period of racial tension in Memphis, where 6 out of 10 Black families lived below the federal poverty line. Large manufacturers like International Harvester and Firestone were hiring Black employees in the 1960s, but they were often systemically discriminated against in terms of pay and working conditions, and their presence was often met with strong resistance

---

38   A Baby Brother's Memories. Notes from Marvin Mims' conversation with Herman Bachus, 2021

from white coworkers and managers. The same year Pastor Bachus was elected pastor at St. Mark, 1966, Black sanitation workers in Memphis attempted their first strike. They had succeeded in getting the American Federation of State, County and Municipal Employees to grant them a union charter, but they struggled to mobilize support for a strike from Memphis' religious community and middle class.[39] Momentum among religious leaders and the city as a whole shifted dramatically in February 1968 after two sanitation workers, Echol Cole and Robert Walker, were crushed to death on the job. Ministers mobilized to join them in demanding change, and Pastor Bachus was among them when Rev. Dr. Martin Luther King Jr. came to Memphis in March 1968 to lead a march in support of the Sanitation Workers' Strike.

Racial tensions during that era made it dangerous for Black preachers to travel. Rev. Dr. Melvin Charles Smith, Senior Pastor of Mount Moriah-East Baptist Church in Memphis, remembers the steps they took to protect each other during this time. "If I was preaching 10 miles north of where Pastor Bachus was preaching, I would wait for him and we would trail each other home," Rev. Dr. Smith said. "We had rendezvous points. It was during the Civil Rights Movement, so we had to exercise discretion in traveling."

---

[39] Memphis Sanitation Workers' Strike. The Martin Luther King Jr. Research and Education Institute, Stanford University. https://kinginstitute.stanford.edu/encyclopedia/memphis-sanitation-workers-strike

Rev. Dr. Smith offered a mini-history lesson on the relationship between Memphis' Black ministers. "There was a class of preachers in Memphis in the 1950s that included Rev. C. L. Franklin, Rev. A. R. Williams, Bishop Gilbert E. Patterson, Rev. A. R. Williams, and Rev. H. H. Harper. Then there was a class of the early 60s that included Rev. William Fields, Rev. Ernest McKinney, Rev. Samuel Billy Kyles, Rev. H. O. Kneeland, Rev. Dr. James Netters, Rev. Oris Mays, and Rev. Ydell Ishmon Sr." The class of preachers in the late 1960s that he and Pastor Bachus belonged to included Rev. Kenneth Whalum Sr., Rev. Dr. James Adams, Rev. Roosevelt Joyner, Rev. Dr. Edward Parker Jr., Rev. Dr. Frank E. Ray, Rev. Dr. David Ricks, and Rev. Andrew Tabor. He reminisced on the strong brotherhood they established.

Rev. Dr. Melvin Charles Smith:

"We were true brothers to each other. One great thing about our era was we prayed and counseled each other. We were not hesitant to seek advice from each other. There were no jealous spirits; we always supported each other. We would drive each other to churches. If one had to preach, another brother drove him to his church appointment. We had real good fellowship. Pastor Bachus helped to organize a breakfast fellowship among his peers. We had a worship fellowship where we exchanged pulpits and a social fellowship. On Sunday nights, we met at one another's house, and

our wives cooked dinner. Our children bonded and knew each other, his children would call me Uncle Melvin, and my children would call him Uncle Johnny.

We would joke and preach what we had preached earlier in the day, sing, and fellowship together. In those days, you had to preach two sermons on Sunday, and you could not preach on Sunday night what you preached on Sunday morning. You either could handle it, or you couldn't handle it. We had kindred experiences and cut our teeth on rural revivals. That was the learning ground. Each church, city, and congregation was different, and we learned how to deal with various congregations.

When we traveled to conventions out of town, we had no hotel reservations. The National Baptist Convention didn't support young preachers, and we couldn't afford suites or hotels, so we would all sleep in one room together. We would sleep in the bed together and even on the floor. On one occasion, Rev. K. T. Whalum, Rev. Luscious Calvin Luther, Pastor Bachus, and I did not have reservations at a hotel. James Brown's band was checking into the hotel, and we pretended to be with the band and got a room. On another occasion, when we were trying to get a hotel room, Pastor Bachus pretended to be my white superior and reprimanded me. He treated me like his servant who forgot to make reservations, and we secured a hotel room. There were numerous times we had to make up stories to get a hotel room. Johnny was in the middle of it all. When we'd *get to a city and not have money to eat at a restaurant, we would go to the grocery store and buy bologna, cheese, and sodas. We had to ride buses or trains wherever we went.*[40]

When Pastor Bachus and Rev. Dr. Smith first met, St. Mark and Mt. Moriah were located near each other in downtown Memphis. Rev. Dr. Smith says that when he told Pastor Bachus in 1972 that he was moving Mt. Moriah from South Orleans Street, a block from Beale Street, to a vacant lot on Haynes Street in a white suburban area, "Pastor Bachus thought I had lost my mind and gone crazy." Since that time, Mt. Moriah has expanded its facilities to include a thousand-seat sanctuary, 2 office wings, classrooms, a 60-seat chapel, and numerous other spaces. Pastor Bachus enjoyed preaching at Mt. Moriah East on many occasions, including anniversary celebrations for Rev. Dr. Smith and his wife, Billie Rutherford Smith. Other churches left the inner city, but Pastor Bachus decided to stay because he felt "the church is needed in the inner city more than anywhere else."[41]

---

[40] Notes from a conversation with Rev. Dr. Melvin Charles Smith, Sr. Pastor, Mt. Moriah-East Baptist Church, Memphis, TN, 2021

[41] Inner City Calls. The Commercial Appeal (Memphis, TN). Thur., March 30, 1995, p. 91.

Pastor Bachus said his greatest accomplishments at St. Mark were "rebuilding the church and building the gym." In 1974, the membership approved a plan to improve the site, which allowed St. Mark to purchase twenty-seven nearby parcels of land. A new sanctuary was built in 1976 and dedicated in 1986 when the mortgage was burned. St. Mark's strong commitment to serving the needs of families was realized in 1988 with the construction of a gymnasium, the J.C. Bachus Multipurpose Building. A new wing was added to the south side of the main sanctuary that houses the pastor's study, an administrative office, a conference room, a classroom, a kitchen, and a dining area.

The old sanctuary was renamed the Rev. B.J. Wilson Fellowship Hall to honor St. Mark MBC's first pastor. A second floor was added in 1990 to the Fellowship Hall to house the Sunday School Department. That same year, the north side of the main sanctuary was remodeled to add seventy-five seats and balance the appearance of the sanctuary.[42] In 2001, the multi-purpose building was expanded to increase the size of the kitchen facilities and dining area.

Pastor Bachus said building the gym was more challenging than building the sanctuary. "Folks were building and remodeling sanctuaries every once in a while, but no one was building a gym. They wanted one

---

42   St. Mark Missionary Baptist Church History, https://stmarkmemphis.wixsite.com/smbcm

but didn't know how to go about it." He used the same contractor for the gym that built the sanctuary.

For 53 years, he led St. Mark in revolutionizing the area on Lauderdale St. and Wicks Ave. His vision and leadership led to much-needed improvements in church facilities, and the gym provided space for St. Mark Sports Ministry and other community and recreational programs. In 1995, St. Mark partnered with the Shelby County Sheriff's Department to sponsor *"No Drugs + No Crime = Freedom Plus a Sound Mind,"* a 10-day anti-drug/anti-crime camp that attracted 1500 youth. Memphis was reeling from the crack cocaine epidemic and gun violence at the time.

Pastor Bachus grew St. Mark MBC from 30 members to a congregation of 600. That growth is also a part of his legacy. Mother Bachus believes that his outgoing, friendly personality and strong relationships with other pastors and churches contributed to St. Mark's growth. She recalls the times when St. Mark fellowshipped with Pastor J. L. Payne, Pastor James Leaks, Pastor W. M. Fields Jr., Pastor Frank E. Ray, Pastor Melvin Charles Smith, Pastor Joseph McGhee, Pastor James Netters, Pastor Kenneth Whalum Sr., and Apostle G. E. Patterson. The Moderator of the Memphis District Association, Pastor O. C. Collins Sr., was one of Pastor Bachus' mentors.

Rev. Dr. David Ricks, Pastor of Robinhood Lane Baptist Church, met Pastor Bachus in the late 1970s. He recalls when he and Pastor Bachus would sit in the back of New Era Baptist Church during Memphis Baptist Pastors Alliance meetings. This was before the Alliance merged with the Baptist Ministers Conference to become the Memphis Baptist Ministerial Association. Pastor Bachus told Rev. Ricks at one meeting, "Why don't these old preachers go somewhere and sit down and let some of us young preachers run things." Years later, Pastor Bachus asked Ricks, "Do you think these young preachers are saying 'Why don't these old preachers go somewhere and sit down, and let us young preachers run things?'"

In April 1981, there were two separate groups for Baptist ministers in Memphis, the Baptist Pastors Alliance and the Baptist Ministers Conference. The two groups had existed for approximately fifty years and were once united. The groups formed a committee to reunite as one organization, and on July 7, 1981, they voted to merge and become the Memphis Baptist Ministerial Association (MBMA). The new organization consisted of 250 ministers and 40 to 50 thousand members.

Pastor Bachus fellowshipped with Baptist ministers every 1st Saturday of the month at a prayer breakfast held at the internationally known Four Way Restaurant and later at the Gay Hawk Restaurant, his favorite place to take Mother Bachus when they were dating.[43] In 1984,

---

[43] In 2021, Pastor Bachus and several other ministers who dined together frequently at Four Way Restaurant were captured in a video celebrating the legendary establishment. The video was created by Google to honor Black businesses during Black History Month. https://youtu.be/EtADTyf5LhM

he was elected President of the Memphis Baptist Ministerial Association, succeeding Rev. V. B. Brown. According to Rev. Ricks, the three things that drew people to Pastor Bachus were his humbleness, generosity, and infectious smile. "When Pastor Bachus served as President of the Memphis Baptist Ministerial Association, he would help any fellow brother preacher in need."

During the year he was president of MBMA, Pastor Bachus was among a small group of influential ministers who met with Memphis Mayor Dennis Hackett to address concerns about the lack of promotional opportunities for African American police officers and firefighters.[44] In 1985, there were no African Americans in command positions in 12 of the city's police departments. The ministers resisted publicizing the meetings out of concern that Hackett would become defensive. He had already rejected the ministers' request to include representatives from the Afro-American Police Association.

Pastor Bachus continued supporting MBMA in many ways long after his presidency. In July 1994, he spoke at New Philadelphia Baptist Church as part of a month-long series of community meetings MBMA sponsored to address crime and violence in Memphis.[45] He also served

---

[44] Chisum, James. (1985) "Talks aimed at promoting black police." The Commercial Appeal (Memphis, TN). Thurs., May 16, 1985, p. 13

[45] "Crime Talk." The Commercial Appeal (Memphis, TN). Fri., January 21, 1994, p16.

as one of the chairpersons for MBMA's yearly revivals and held other leadership roles as Moderator of the Memphis District Association, and Dean of City Union # 2,[46] and was involved with many other religious organizations in Memphis and the State of Tennessee.

Pastor Bachus conducted revivals in California, Texas, Oklahoma, New York, Michigan, Ohio, Louisiana, and other places in the U.S., leading to innumerable souls being converted, revived, and healed in the name of Jesus. "I preached in almost every state in the Union," he said. "I can't say how well I preached, but I can say I preached."[47]

Bachus' powerful preaching was my reason for following him all across the city to hear him preach at various churches. According to Rev. Dr. Smith, "Pastor Bachus did not attend seminary like many, but he had a God-given theology and he was a common-sense preacher. Wherever Pastor Bachus went he would lift the crowd. He would lift a crowd at Metropolitan like he would at St. Mark. It did not matter if they were learned or unlearned, he could lift a crowd. Pastor Bachus loved people. When he went to a pulpit, he did not go being pious, he

---

[46] City Union is a group of Baptist churches that are part of the Memphis Baptist Ministerial Association, and provide Christian missions locally within their churches and support our State Convention. We meet monthly at various churches for preaching, teaching, fellowship, and to report on what member churches are doing locally in the work of the ministry of Christ.

[47] Notes from Rev. Marvin Mims' conversation with Rev. Dr. Johnny C. Bachus, June 20, 2020

Rev. Dr. Johnny Clarence ("J.C.") Bachus

went low and when he went low, the low took him high. When he got finished preaching it was like First Baptist Rome, with high-spirited preaching and praise."[48]

Rev. Ricks offered the same kind of praise, describing him as a Preacher's Preacher. "Pastor Bachus knew when to go deep in his preaching and when to stay shadow based on the congregation he was preaching to. If it was an educated church, he could go high. If it was a common church, he would go low. He knew how to communicate with people on their level. He preached to people where they were." His style of preaching was to open with a song before taking a text that was inspirational to many people. Ricks believed the song was sung to lead into the sermon Bachus was preaching. Pastor Bachus had a passion for ministry and music. "He was a preacher that could sing and not a singing preacher."

On November 9, 1980, the St. Mark Missionary Baptist Church Mass, Choir recorded the album "Closer to Jesus." The album, which was recorded live and mastered at Nashville Record Productions (NR12301), includes three songs written by Pastor Bachus: *"I'm Going Over," "Hallelujah, I've Been Saved,"* and *"Closer to Jesus."*

---

[48] Notes from a conversation with Rev. Dr. Melvin Charles Smith, Sr. Pastor, Mt. Moriah-East Baptist Church, Memphis, TN, 2021

In addition to his leadership roles with local and statewide organizations, Pastor Bachus also served as a board member of the National Baptist Convention, USA, Inc. Founded in 1886, the National Baptist Convention, USA, Inc. is the nation's oldest and largest African American religious organization with an estimated membership of 7.5 million individuals and 30,000 congregations. The Convention's annual meeting typically attracts 20,000 attendees. During the President's Hour of the Convention's 2014 Annual Meeting, which was held in New Orleans, Pastor Bachus was one of those honored for 50 years of continuous service as a pastor. "As time moved on, God blessed Pastor Bachus to grow from rural preaching to being the main speaker at the National Baptist Convention, USA, Inc.," said longtime friend Rev. Dr. Smith who is now an internationally recognized evangelist. "When we both made it on the big stage there was no pompous, just gratitude. In later years when we went to the National Convention, we laughed at the times we got put out of churches for being loud!"

Pastor Bachus was very humble. He didn't talk much about his achievements so pulling together those threads of his life was a challenge. He was so humble that it wasn't until after he passed that I found his Master in Biblical Studies degree in the Pastor's office at St. Mark. He earned the degree in 2007 from Brewster Theological Clinic and School of Religion. Dr. Samuel Turner was President at that time. Brewster Theological Clinics were founded by Rev. Dr. William Herbert Brewster, Pastor of East Trigg Avenue Baptist Church and one of America's most prominent Black ministers, composers, theologians, and community leaders. Rev. Dr. Brewster recognized the need to provide educational opportunities for Black ministers, so he established Brewster Theological Clinics in Memphis and other cities. He was also one of the founders of the Tennessee School of Religion.

It's not uncommon for people to question the validity of a Black minister's credentials. *Who ordained him? What kind of school did he attend? Why do so many black preachers call themselves doctor?* The history of Black theological education is, in many ways, the story of our struggle and survival in America. Let us not forget there was a time when it was against the law for African Americans to get any kind of education, nonetheless one that taught them how to inspire and lead others. There was a time when white people feared African Americans gathering for ANY purpose, including praising God in a way that reflected our customs, shared experiences, and needs. We weren't allowed to educate or lift ourselves up without permission.

The religious education institutions that African American ministers and Theologians created, such as Brewster Theological Clinic and School of Religion and the Tennessee School of Religion, should always be placed within the context of the critical role they've played in the growth and development of Black religious leaders. The diplomas and degrees earned from these institutions attest to a person attaining a level of biblical and theoretical knowledge. They're not intended to represent or replace the academic courses of study people receive at colleges and universities that award BA/BS, Masters, and Doctoral degrees. Having attended the Tennessee School of Religion myself, I appreciate its history, purpose, and value. I knew preaching would require more biblical study and formal education, and I received a solid foundation there.

Without question, Rev. Dr. J. C. Bachus earned the Honorary Doctorate degree in Divinity, Humanities and Humane Letters he received from the Tennessee School of Religion in 1992. While raising a beloved family, he dedicated his life to preaching God's words, bringing compassionate spiritual relief to generations of weary souls, and mentoring, training, organizing, and leading Black ministers.

Something about Pastor Bachus stood out for me in writing this book, a unique and powerful thread that wound its way through his entire life. That thread was Pastor Bachus' unwavering and unapologetic support of Black institutions, communities, and businesses. From taking courses at LeMoyne-Owen College, one of the nation's Historically Black Colleges and Universities, raising his family in a subdivision built by a Black entrepreneur, and patronizing Black businesses like Four

Way Restaurant, to immersing himself in curricula created and taught by Black theologians and working tirelessly to strengthen the fellowship among Black preachers, Pastor Bachus spent his life championing the tradition of African Americans educating and uplifting themselves. In a nutshell, he believed in and loved his people.

Pastor Bachus had a remarkable partner on his journey, his beautiful wife of 63 years, John Ella Bachus. As the pastor's wife, she was expected to be at St. Mark whenever the doors were open. This is sometimes an undue burden the pastor or church may place upon the pastor's wife. She sacrificed whatever personal ambitions she may have had to support Pastor Bachus' ministry. Church members often flock to the pastor after worship, while his wife receives very little recognition. The Pastor gets the glory and walks home with the trophy when his wife is the backbone of his ministry. She is the one watching his blind spots and analyzing his decisions to stop him from entering the danger zone of criticism. She often keeps things together at home while the pastor visits the sick and shut-in. The Pastor's wife is usually the primary encourager, picking him up on those Sundays when a sermon didn't get off the runway, nonetheless into the air. She strokes his ego at home, telling him he is doing a good job when he is struggling to survive. Mother Bachus served as an encourager and a prayer warrior for Pastor Bachus, and her prayers are so powerful and spiritual that you would almost want her to pray for you rather than the Pastor! She was a quiet, respectful, and dignified First Lady, always peaceful, never argumentative with Pastor Bachus, in public or with the congregation. St. Mark always viewed her as an impeccable First Lady because of her humility, spirituality, style, and grace.

Anita Bachus Mims:

"As a girl, I saw my mother care for her family in many ways. She always prepared breakfast and dinner. I tried to help, and sometimes I watched her around the house when I wasn't at school or napping. My favorite meal was on Wednesdays. Mom would cook cornbread, Pinto beans, and fried chicken. I never wrote down her recipes, but I learned them by memory. She taught me everything about being a good homemaker. Once I learned how to iron, I would iron all my dad's shirts and handkerchiefs. Mom showed joy in doing what she did for her family. As a teenager and the only girl growing up in the home, I was given a room to myself, and my brothers had to share a room. I often redecorate my room, and my brothers got jealous, but soon appreciated my skills. Watching my mom helped me to learn how to organize and maintain a safe and clean home.

The First Lady is often overlooked because most people love their Pastor and look to him for guidance. Of course, some crush on their pastor, especially if he's smart and good-looking. I think if a First lady is quiet, people don't think she has any input, but it's wisdom. I watched my mom for most of my life and paid attention to how she was treated and how she treated others. Many treated her very kindly, while there were a few that didn't. She always treated people with kindness and a smile. She stayed focused on her calling, which was to serve in the ministry of Jesus Christ and to be a help-mate to her husband."[49]

Pastor Bachus embodied the positive traits of a father and was a great role model for dads. He was a genuinely caring and concerned father who lovingly nurtured his children and grandchildren. He became a father-in-law and grandfather more rapidly than expected when Anita and I married so young, and she gave birth to his first granddaughter Takenya. He showed love and affection to his extended family, which included in-laws, grandchildren, and great-grandchildren. I was proud to call him Dad.

He had a unique way of dropping wise tips for righteous living on his children and grandchildren during family holiday celebrations or reunions. Pastor Bachus and Mother Bachus hosted family holiday celebrations at their home for decades, something his children, grandchildren, great-grandchildren, and a host of relatives have treasured down through the years. Christmas was a time of feasting on

---

[49] A personal reflection on her mother, John Ella Bachus. Anita Bachus Mims, 2021

a fabulous dinner prepared primarily by Mother Bachus, known for her delicious burnt roast. Additional family members contribute with their best dish, and the family participates in gift-giving, singing, watching sports, playing games, guitar and piano playing, and joke-telling. Pastor Bachus was the main comedian; he'd have us laughing all over the place. He often inserted humorous church jokes in the mix, sometimes about church members but never using real names.

Growing up, I admired Coach Eddie Robinson, the legendary coach of Grambling State University's football team for 56 years. Coach Robinson brought fame and success to the Southwestern Athletic Conference, which consisted of Historical Black Colleges and Universities in the Southern part of the United States. Pastor Bachus reminded me of Coach Robinson in a way. He was the legendary Pastor of St. Mark who led the church for 53 years. A great coach knows his players, a great Pastor knows his members, and a great Dad knows his children. He often encouraged family members to stick together, love one another, practice forgiveness, and recognize the good in one another. He was the ultimate counselor who shared practical tips for living based on life experiences and knowing people are human, imperfect, and sinful. There is no record of Pastor Bachus expressing anger with his children or grandchildren, only patience and love.

He loved his grandchildren and gave them all unique nicknames like Gooba, Spacey, Takanaka, Pug, Popeye, Rodney June Bug, Pawncey Wancy, RL, and Fat Jaws, just to name a few. He made time for them and included them in conversations at the dinner table. He was the same with children in the church, laughing and joking with them and never pushing them away.

Takenya Mims:

"Grandad always made time for us (grandkids). I would like to think I got the most time since I am the 2nd grandchild, but that would be far from the truth. He spent as much time with all of us as he possibly could. Any events he was aware of, if he didn't have previous obligations, he would show up. A lot of times, other commitments didn't stop him. He simply did them all by managing and prioritizing his time. He showed me early on that if a person wants to truly be there for you, they will! Grandad was such a great family man and patriarch for our family. His greatness was not only for us to see, but he exuded that same energy with the church, St. Mark. He showed me in so many ways what humbleness, meekness, kindness, and temperance meant in human form. All the grandkids had nicknames ordained by him, lol. Many people would try and call me his special name and I would correct them quickly. That was and will always be reserved just for him.

Grandad was a man of many skills. He could sing, teach, preach, work with his hands, counsel, and play the guitar. My love for music, singing, and preaching sincerely runs deep. It is truly in my blood; matter of fact, it is within all of us. We are a talented bunch of grandkids, and we genuinely get it honest! I have always cherished him and our relationship, and I cherish it even more now that he's no longer physically present. His name, J. C. Bachus, has so much clout, respect, and dignity tied to it. He will always be a legend in our family and in Memphis."[50]

Tracy Ann Walker:

"Granddaddy or Spandaddy, as I call him, holds the dearest place in my heart. Ever since I can remember, he has always been there. Steadfast and statutory in my life. He was a public figure that we could see backstage, and his walk and talk always lined up. He was noble and admired by all my friends and everyone I knew. I guess it came from his humor and friendliness. He always seemed to make people feel welcome and important. No matter if you were a 3-year-old, man, woman, teen, elderly, stranger, or family member, your life mattered to him.

He passed out nicknames like pieces of candy. Everyone got one, Lol, especially the kids. Mine was Spacey, and I, in turn, called him Spandaddy. It's funny because our secret nickname for me was Favorite.

---

[50] A personal reflection on her grandfather Rev. Dr. J. C. Bachus, Takenya Mims, 2021

Haha! I always tried to make him admit that I was his favorite grandchild, and even though I knew he loved us all the same, he would still jokingly call me his favorite, and we'd laugh in our private moments.

Granddaddy Bachus is the funniest person you could meet. He always has a quick rebuttal or snap-back that you never see coming. Many times, he would joke right along with the grandkids, making us feel that we could truly be ourselves around him. But we never lost our respect. We knew that he was called and a man of God first. He wanted to know if we were saved and if we knew the word. That mattered to him. It mattered to him where we were every Sunday morning (and Wednesday nights lol).

When I first left St. Mark to find 'more,' I was around 21. And even as an adult, he never stopped asking me to come back home. Home was St. Mark. He made it home. He was always there! Whenever I would dial 901-774-2427, he was sure to answer! He was dedicated to the ministry and not just the word of God, but the whole life experience. We would travel together on church trips, serve the community together, play sports together, eat together, and go to each other's homes. He found a way to encompass all of life's joys into the church.

My best memories are, of course, Christmas time when we would wake up at 4 a.m. and go to church. We would have Christmas service early. It would always be dark and intimate because only a few church members would come to the 5 a.m. service. But we would be there and afterward head to our aunts for breakfast. We would ALL be there, cousins and aunts and uncles and grandad and Grandma.

Last, we would be at their house for dinner and presents. We all knew what was coming! Money! Grandad gave each and every kid money! It was the best. Because after we had racked up numerous gifts from everyone, he would give the last and final gift. Money! And we were all so excited to get it.

Grandad made us respect him even more because of the way he treated Grandma. There was always love and respect in how he treated her. He never disrespected her in front of us. It was such a solid foundation for our family. He was such a solid foundation. His smile is so settling that it makes you feel like everything is alright, even if you are dealing with so much at the time. His words were always so full of wisdom and yet simplistic. Applicable wisdom. I love talking to him and I love sitting under him. Whenever I could be around him, I just soaked up each moment. I knew then and now that I was in the presence of greatness.

Granddaddy is a preacher's preacher. He could sing and preach and squall and dance, all while in his cowboy boots. Many imitated his style, but he was the original. His voice was stellar too. He recorded albums and his favorite was quartet style, something he passed down to his grandkids too. We loved to sing, especially the girls. We formed a quartet group called the Sistas and we would practice and sing at the church. Grandad could play piano and guitar, but his main instrument was his voice. His song was 'Wonderful.' He was known for it and people couldn't wait for him to sing it.

I can still hear the screams of church members shouting and crying after he bellows out, "It is no secret, what God can do!" Followed by his laugh, 'Hahahaha!' Because he too was happy, singing about the joy of Jesus. Once at Christmas, I sang 'Wonderful' for him and he cried. It was a moment I will always cherish because I think he knew then that he had lived a life of legacy. And that legacy won't soon be forgotten. Because he was watching it then and there: in his kids, in his grandkids, in his music, in his ministry. We all carried it and we all can thank him for that."[51]

On November 6, 2018, the Memphis City Council approved a street name change to honor Pastor Bachus, and on January 11, 2019, City officials, St. Mark's congregation, family, friends, and the community gathered to celebrate when the section that runs from South Lauderdale and E. H. Crump Boulevard to Lauderdale Street and Walker Avenue was renamed "Rev. J. C. Bachus Boulevard."

November 2019 marked the 53rd year of Rev. Dr. Bachus faithfully pastoring St. Mark Missionary Baptist Church. During his selection, no one envisioned him growing a small membership into a

---

[51] A personal reflection on her grandfather Rev. Dr. J. C. Bachus, Tracy Ann Walker, 2021

vibrant congregation of 600 people and transforming the intersection of Wicks and Lauderdale St. Under his leadership, the church was blessed spiritually, physically, and economically, and grew in size and influence. Rev. Bachus also produced several ministers who are spreading God's word, including me. On October 27, 2019, he passed the torch into my hands as the new Pastor of St. Mark, incorporating a vision "to become a first-class Church for ministry, healing, help, and wholeness for Memphis families." I CORINTHIANS 12:28.[52]

---

[52] St. Mark Missionary Baptist Church History, https://stmarkmemphis.wixsite.com/smbcm

CHAPTER SEVEN

The Crossroads of Champions

Anyone who has ever gone through the fire knows how much it changes you to come out whole on the other side. I went through the fire in the decade leading up to my departure from the military. I had risen to the rank of Chief Master Sergeant but not without enduring the hardship of racial discrimination. I had fought and won numerous battles, but even in victory, racism leaves scars. From the squalor of housing settlements in South Africa to substandard living conditions in Foote Homes, a public housing community intentionally built to segregate poor blacks in Memphis, I'd witnessed poverty's devastating, long-term impact. I experienced the magnificence of the Holy Spirit's compelling force when I was called to preach and the depression and emotional toll that came when Land on the Rock Ministry failed. Needless to say, I wasn't the same kid who'd left Greenville, Mississippi in 1978 to start a new life in Memphis, a kid who felt victorious when my cousin Dewey let me drive his purple muscle car.

Another cousin, Kent "Bruno" Russell, was also a champion in my life. Growing up, we were close and as adults, we raised our children together. His father was my favorite Uncle Jake. In 2012, after I retired from the military and returned to St. Mark, Kent and I had discussions about going into business together. We thought it was a good time to reopen Bruno's, an Italian restaurant he owned a few years earlier. He opened the original Bruno's in the Mid-town area of Memphis in 2008. It was a unique family-style Italian restaurant, one of few Black-owned dining establishments in Memphis and the *only* Black-owned Italian restaurant. Kent believed he was destined to open an Italian restaurant because his aunt Dorothy Green (his mother's sister) gave him the middle name Bruno.

People came from all around Memphis to enjoy his delicious cooking. Bruno's was largely family-operated, with his son Addison serving as an excellent cook as well. A feature story in the *Commercial Appeal* newspaper helped to promote the business.[53] The restaurant offered an informal atmosphere where people came for intimate dinners, family gatherings, wedding parties, graduations, and other special occasions. It was also a popular lunch spot. Anita and I were blessed to be investors in Bruno's and contribute to Kent's dream being

---

53   Koeppel, Frederic. "Bruno's Italian Restaurant offers tasty, affordable meals, friendly service." Commercial Appeal. September 21, 2007. https://archive.commercialappeal.com/entertainment/brunos-italian-restaurant-offers-tasty-affordable-meals-friendly-service-ep-398878249-323991531.html/

realized. It always concerned us that there were very few black-owned, full-service restaurants in Memphis. Kent's dad lived to see it come to fruition as well, and his mother, Justine Russell, and our entire family were extremely happy and proud of his being a successful and rising entrepreneur.

Bruno's held special memories of the fulfillment of a field of dreams, Kent's, ours, and so many others. A special memory Kent, Anita, and I share was the night President Obama won the 2008 election. It meant a lot to us that we were standing in a Black-owned Italian restaurant rejoicing together.

I never saw anyone work so hard and be so committed to excellence as my cousin Kent. He devoted his heart and soul to Bruno's, but the restaurant only survived two years. It was hard to overcome the economic downturn of the Great Recession of 2008. When the restaurant failed, we talked about forming another partnership. Now that I had retired from the Air Force, we felt it was time to implement the dream.

Kent and I searched all over the city for the best location to reopen Bruno's. We found a building in a high-traffic area in Bartlett we thought would be an ideal location. We met with the owner of the building, negotiated a lease contract, and began the process of obtaining licenses to reopen Bruno's. We were extremely excited and felt the potential was unlimited. Bartlett did not have an Italian restaurant near the main business section of the city. With only a few Black-owned restaurants in town, we thought we would get a lot of Black support, especially with Shelby County being the largest county out of 95 counties in Tennessee.

After obtaining all of the required licenses and cleaning the building extensively, we opened the doors on November 12, 2012. We got off to a slow start, but within a month, business was booming. Before opening, we hired a staff of diverse young people and gave them extensive training. It was truly a family business. My oldest daughter Takenya was an excellent manager during weeknights and weekends, my daughter Tracy managed our financial accounting records and monitored our expenses, and Joshua, my son-in-law, assisted on some weekends with cooking. Kent and I treated our other staff like family and had a great relationship with them. Most of the time, we were relaxed with our employees, but we had to discipline them sometimes with a verbal warning, letter of reprimand, or termination. It wasn't easy, but we did it. We fired one employee but rehired her later because of her outstanding service and personality and our desire to give people a second chance. Anita was on call whenever I needed an extra server, which was often in our early days. Everyone loved her personality, and she often received large amounts of gratuity. One of our regular white male customers routinely gave Anita $20 when she approached the table to serve him and his African American wife. This shocked Anita because he blessed her with those generous tips before she started serving them! She maintained excellent customer service skills from serving as a waitress early in our marriage. She would help as a host by greeting guests and making them feel welcome as she seated them. She never complained when she had to purchase grocery items we needed at the produce market or grocery store. I occasionally tipped her myself just to let her know how much Kent and I appreciated her help.

After Bruno's was featured in the weekly *Memphis Flyer* newspaper, customers stormed our business for months. We had repeat customers who boasted about the food and service, including one couple who dined with us 4 or 5 times a week. They spent generously and did all they could to help us to succeed. Families held small and large gatherings there, and we became a popular spot for wedding and birthday celebrations and graduation parties. Kent and I established relationships with many city officials, pastors in Bartlett, and churches who supported our business. There were no financial worries during our first year of business.

It brought me gratitude that we were training young people to serve and operate a business, which they did whenever Kent and I couldn't be there. Our employees had great people skills and knew how to function under pressure and handle dissatisfied customers. We treated our customers with the utmost respect and made sure they received a high-quality experience when they visited Bruno's.

During lunch one day, I met a wonderful lady, Donna Davenport, a member of Sycamore View Church of Christ. Anita and I developed a great friendship with Mrs. Davenport. We visited her church occasionally and met her husband, pastor, and several church members. She frequently scheduled staff luncheons at Bruno's and had us cater events at her church. Sycamore View Church of Christ wholeheartedly supported us and treated us like members. People like Mrs. Davenport and others made us feel appreciated in our efforts to maintain our business. I am blessed to still have her as a friend.

I quickly learned that in business, you do what you have to do to survive, legally that is, so I learned how to make mixed drinks, not the norm for a Baptist preacher! We wined and dined our customers, providing them with great service, good food, beer, wine, and mixed drinks. Our first year was a huge success. We didn't have any financial problems that year. However, during our second year, Bruno's experienced a significant downturn. Our customer base did not expand, existing customers began to vanish, and our business dried up like someone had bombed the building. We kept searching for answers on how we could make the restaurant more popular and grow our customer base. We tried numerous things to revive the business, such as adding live entertainment, painting the restaurant building, modifying the menu, and installing a kiosk machine to offer discounts. Our new ideas did not produce sustained success.

Kent poured his heart and soul into trying to make the business thrive, working 70 hours a week, and I poured a lot of cash into it, robbing Peter to pay Paul. Anita and I used all our financial resources to pay debts and meet employee payroll. We cut back hours and positions where we could, but that only put a band-aid on our problem.

We struggled to understand why our business was going downhill if people loved Bruno's food so much. One theory was that we were operating in a predominately white area. Kent and I had heated discussions about why we were sinking and how money should be spent, and I would leave the building to avoid making matters worse. Yet, after a day or two, we would reunite like a married couple and work as one to come up with more ideas to make the restaurant succeed.

We had mounting expenses operating in an old building and constant maintenance issues with the deep freezer, oven, vented hood, ice machine, plumbing, and central air conditioning. The only thing that didn't break in the building was Kent's spirit and mine.

None of the employees knew about our real financial struggle, so when we finally announced the restaurant's closing, some were surprised and saddened. I was relieved because I was swimming in debt and about to drown. I understood from this experience why people commit suicide after a failed business, not that I entertained the idea. Anita and I were losing $6,000 a month with fourteen months left on the building lease agreement. This extremely challenging experience taught me many valuable business lessons, one being to consult an attorney in business negotiations rather than act like one myself.

Our lessor often forgot we paid him part of the rent on the 1st of the month. He would haggle us over the rent, even though we always paid the late fee. One day his son called me and was upset about us not paying the full amount on the first day of the month. I told him I own real estate and if someone does not pay my rent, I accept the late fee and don't make a big deal out of it if they pay each month. Our lessor's son got angry and asked me if I wanted out of the lease. I told him, "Yes," and based on that conversation, I drafted a one-page lease termination contract I found online, which I let my attorney review. When my attorney gave his approval to the lease termination contract, I believed it was going to be our exit ticket! God had miraculously provided a way of escape.

I was shocked when the lessor and his son tried to renege on our agreement. They lied and said we did not agree on a lease termination contract. I could understand the lessor making this statement because he had dementia, but his son was straight-up lying. After this, I refused to pay any more rent and took the chance on them suing me. I didn't have a leg to stand on in a court of law, but I took the chance anyway. Then one morning, a Ford 150 truck pulled into my driveway as I was leaving my house. It was our lessor's son. He jumped out of his truck and approached me to ask why I was not paying rent. When I told him I would no longer pay rent because he and his father lied about the lease termination contract, the son agreed on the spot to accept the contract. We met a few days later, and all parties signed the contract. When the lessor asked me if my attorney had written the contract, I said yes. I drew up the contract, but he probably felt I was not intelligent enough to accomplish such a task as a Black man, so I let him think a lawyer had done it. The contract released us from the lease within 30 days, and we paid $12,000 for the buyout option. In August 2014, we closed the business.

Bruno's still owed Shelby County $4,900 in taxes for leasing the property. I included a payment plan for the property taxes owed to Shelby County in the lease termination contract. After making all the tax payments for six months, the lessor paid the last tax payment. I was surprised he paid the final tax bill for $700.00. I did not think much about it until my doorbell rang a few weeks later, and a Shelby County Sherriff delivered a summons to court. The lessor was suing us for $10,000 for failing to pay taxes on the property we leased from him. This shocked me even further and caused me to realize we had been in business with a father and son who were deceitful and greedy. I immediately discussed the lawsuit with my attorney and provided him with receipts and documentation showing I had paid all the taxes we were obligated to pay. My attorney said he would contact the plaintiff's attorney and investigate the matter. My attorney successfully resolved the matter in court, and I did not have to appear in court and only owed $700.00. It was good riddance of this corruption scheme for me.

A parting blessing for Kent was he would meet a beautiful, spirited woman named Denina (DJ) a few months before we closed Bruno's and would later marry her. I was blessed to perform the ceremony. At the close of our business, Kent found joy with his new bride.

Despite everything that had happened with Land on the Rock Ministry and Bruno's, I knew there was so much more for me to accomplish in life. After closing the restaurant, I began to attend St. Mark on a more regular basis. I later enrolled in Webster University's graduate degree program in Management and Leadership. I considered attending Memphis Theological Seminary, but at that point in life, I was less interested in earning a degree in theology, which required significantly more research. I just wanted a smooth path to get paid my military education benefits.

The Crossroads of Champions

I always enjoyed the challenge of academic studies that made me think critically and grow spiritually. At Webster University, I enjoyed a great learning environment and great instructors. A few instructors had strong political beliefs that suggested the country was in a downward spiral because President Obama was in the White House. They openly discussed their belief in capitalism and concerns about the government heading down a path of socialism. Discussions often centered around immigration and government socialism, code language for minorities receiving benefits at taxpayer expenses. They complained about the high corporate tax system in the U.S., which was reduced years later by another president in a way that did not benefit the average employee nearly as much as it did corporations and shareholders. Some students agreed with these lies and myths, but I held on to my views about the rich getting richer in America and our need to do more to help the poor, especially children who can't help themselves. I challenged some instructors on issues of low minimum wages and corporate greed. During the presidential election of 2016, I had an instructor who was certain #45 would be great for the country based on his success in business. I took a lot of classes with an African American woman who was in the same graduate program. The two of us didn't hold back in disagreeing with our instructor's thoughts on #45, and time would prove us right. As #45 quickly discovered, running a business (in his case, sometimes into the ground) and running a bureaucracy as large and complex as the U.S. federal government are not the same. We weren't the only ones who felt this way since #45 lost his re-election bid.

Two female instructors stood out during my studies at Webster University. Ms. Stokes was a great teacher who had a friendly personality. She was flexible and very knowledgeable about workplace dynamics, which she integrated into her teaching methods. She had students work in teams to create written lesson plans and teach a textbook chapter. It would always amaze me how two or three people did most of the work in every group, and some groups did not function well because of slackers. In Ms. Stokes' courses, I was always blessed to be part of a productive group with maybe one slacker. She was committed to helping students overcome their fears of communicating in public and developing them into spokespersons and leaders who take the initiative.

Mrs. Camp, the other exceptional teacher, was highly motivated and had a unique teaching style. She taught business principles and stressed to her students the dangers of being in debt. I particularly enjoyed her lectures on different leadership traits. Mrs. Camp shared many presentations about consumer buying habits and marketing strategies for selling to consumers. One of the presentations, *The Secret of Selling to The Negro*, is a classic short film produced over fifty years ago by Johnson Publishing Company, publisher of *Ebony* and *Jet* magazines.[54] It was interesting to see that corporate America was interested in the buying power of African Americans long before many of us had the right to vote.

Through my studies at Webster University, I was exposed to different models and theories about leadership in government and business and different leadership styles. I learned how great leaders accomplish great things through people. While taking these courses, I started associating every topic with St. Mark. In many ways, I could relate my studies with what was happening at St. Mark, with what our church needed.

I thought about how St. Mark had always been a progressive and growing church, but it was becoming stagnant. The high praise St. Mark was known for under Pastor Bachus had begun to diminish among the members. There were no community outreach programs like in the past with the baseball team, basketball league, and Sports Ministry. I saw St. Mark's youth were less committed and only supported the church during the annual Youth Day or Youth 4th Sundays. There was a lack of training and development for the next generation of leaders to ensure they could sustain our progress. I saw the same people in the same positions for 30 years or more without anything new being offered.

---

54   1954, February 1. The Secret of Selling the Negro. Film. Johnson Publishing Company. https://www.c-span.org/video/?508619-1/the-secret-selling-negro

I took a course with the Dean, and he required us to read a book entitled *Our Iceberg is Melting: Changing and Succeeding Under Any Conditions*.[55] I saw St. Mark in the book from start to finish. The book tells a fable about a colony of penguins living on an iceberg that is melting, but one penguin discovers the problem. There were some penguins in denial about their predicament. Different penguins represent people who are part of an organization: the observer, the thinker, the doubter, the communicator, the researcher, the organizer, and the leader. To survive, the penguins living on the melting iceberg eventually had to recognize their problem, develop a strategy, and plan for a new way of living. The book's premise is that change is hard, and we often deny we need to change even when it's necessary to survive. This is where I saw St. Mark. We were faltering like the melting iceberg, but no one would say so, and some refused to recognize it.

My graduate paper, *"Why Organizations Refuse to Accept Change When Change is Necessary for Survival,"* was written with St. Mark at the forefront of my thoughts. Subconsciously, I was asking myself, "What is my role in all of this?" It was as though God was preparing me to lead the church, but that was not my ambition. After going through the fire of having to close Bruno's, I was finally enjoying life and my retirement from the military, especially spending time with my precious grandson

---

55   Kotter, John and Holder Rathgeber. Our Iceberg is Melting: Changing and Succeeding Under Any Conditions. New York: St. Martin's Press. 2006

Hazen. Hazen brought great joy to our family as the first grandchild. We cherish him as a grandson, but we've had the privilege of raising him like a son. Marvin Jr. was a gift after we lost Travis, but Hazen was an extra special gift, and I loved the freedom of traveling down the highway with his Nene (Anita) to visit him.

In the words of one of my many wise good friends, Arthur Martin, "Life is good!" Why would I volunteer to help solve a huge problem that wasn't mine? Why would I give up the life of freedom to lead another church? Our children had moved to Houston, Texas, and in the minds of many, we were only steps away from relocating there as well. The only thing that kept us back was Pastor and Mrs. Bachus and our concern and care for them. Still, I continued learning things in my coursework at Webster that revealed why things were happening at St. Mark, and heading towards graduation, I was still asking myself what my role was in all of this.

I completed my studies at Webster and graduated in May 2017. At my graduation party, one of my best friends, Pastor Ronald Hampton, stated in front of family, friends, and members of St. Mark, that if something was to happen to him, he had instructed his church to appoint me as the pastor. Pastor Hampton had shared this with me on many occasions and even with his congregation, but this time St. Mark heard it. It showed how Right Direction Christian Ministries (RDCM) members and our extended church family held Anita and me in high esteem. Anita and I always enjoyed worshipping with RDCM, sharing in their powerful praise and Pastor Hampton's anointed preaching. Looking in the rearview mirror, God was preparing me to lead St. Mark, implement change, and lead the church during a pandemic.

Several months passed at St. Mark, and we noticed an even more significant loss in members. I had a personal meeting with Pastor Bachus in his study and humbly asked him if he considered retiring at some point. I did it out of concern for his legacy and the welfare of the church. Pastor Bachus listened intently but did not voice his plans with me. He always prayed about major decisions and never made them hastily, so I wasn't surprised he did not respond immediately to my question. He would wait on the Lord to guide him. I continued supporting him and St. Mark. It was difficult at times because I had studied change in graduate school, and everything I learned helped me understand the challenges at St. Mark.

Rev. Casey, Pastor Bachus' nephew, was also in conversation with him about his plans for leadership succession. By the power of the Holy Spirit, after several meetings, Rev. Casey was able to help persuade Pastor Bachus that it was in St. Mark's best interest for him to appoint a new pastor because the church was waiting on his decision on a successor. That same year, in 2017, Pastor Bachus' children, daughters-in-law, and son-in-law had a family meeting with him to encourage him to consider a retirement date. It was an emotional meeting. He felt strongly about his ability to continue functioning as Pastor of St. Mark. The family supported his decision while continuing to pray for him to yield to the Holy Spirit and transfer leadership at St. Mark.

Two years after the family meeting, Pastor Bachus decided it was time for him to transfer leadership. On October 27, 2019, before morning worship, the Holy Spirit moved on his heart. During morning worship, when Pastor Bachus announced to the congregation he was retiring, there was an outcry of weeping and rejoicing among the members like we had never witnessed before. The parishioners rejoiced because Pastor Bachus had faithfully fulfilled his assignment from God to lead St. Mark and served with great distinction and honor. Everyone knew Pastor Bachus had poured his heart, soul, mind, and body into St. Mark for five decades, and his charismatic leadership had elevated St. Mark to lofty heights among the Christian community in Memphis. He was one of the longest-serving pastors in Memphis. Nevertheless, just as Moses had to relinquish the reins of leadership to Joshua, so did Pastor Bachus relinquish the leadership of St. Mark. He had taken St. Mark as far as he could. In the words of the Apostle Paul, "He had finished his course." It was as though a burden had been released over the church, empowering St. Mark to move forward into the future.

After the celebration and rejoicing, he appointed me to lead the church. I think in many people's minds, they questioned what my leading the church would look like. Was it temporary leadership or permanent? It was an enormous transition for Pastor Bachus, and he would gradually yield power to me. Initially, Pastor Bachus still decided who would preach, led prayer in his office before worship, and gave pastoral comments during Sunday school. I allowed him that time to adjust; it was a blessing because I was not thrust into the limelight. The gradual change was easier for everyone to accept, and it gave me time to grow into being the new pastor. I remember Anita being so relieved she wept with joy. She had personal conversations with her father regarding this decision. For some strange reason, I shed few tears, if any, but I was greatly relieved because I knew this was the best thing for Pastor Bachus and the church.

I realized that what I considered failures with Land on the Rock Ministry and Bruno's Restaurant were steps on the road to leading St. Mark. The work I had done to improve the lives of the poor in our community was all in preparation to receive the blessing passed down from Pastor Bachus. On the fourth Sunday of October 2019, during the worship hour, I stood at one of the most significant crossroads in my life when a true champion, Rev. Dr. J. C. Bachus, transferred the leadership of the church he had led for over 50 years to me.

Pastor Bachus was a strong leader who never surrendered to a spiritual fight. When he retired from leading St. Mark, it was a day of rejoicing. God had given him the strength to say, "I have been a good and faithful servant, I have served faithfully and it's someone's else's time." The Lord had lifted a heavy burden off Pastor Bachus' mind and spirit with this decision, and he became more joyful during times of worship and Sunday school. I cherish the times we laughed and joked about the transition. After a few months, I offered to give him his church back because he was in a different place spiritually, but he declined the offer. When I offered to give him his daughter back and said I had taken care of Anita for 40 years, he declined that offer, too!

CHAPTER EIGHT

Pastor, Priest & Prophet

I was blessed to have Pastor Bachus lay hands on me one Sunday morning during his transition of leadership. His hands were held up by Deacon Preston Pittman and Rev. Dan Greer. During my installation, Pastor Vernon Horner, former President of the Memphis Baptist Ministerial Association, laid hands on me and prayed for me at the altar. It was an honor to have these great men of God lay hands on me and pray for my success in doing the work God had called me to accomplish. They knew the hills and valleys in the road ahead.

During his 53 years leading St. Mark, Pastor Bachus accumulated a wealth of knowledge about the nuances of pastoral leadership. I can't place a value on the lessons I received from him about being a pastor, but I can pass along the blessings by sharing some of them here.

How does a pastor maintain a solid and healthy congregation for over fifty years? Pastor Bachus believed it begins with the disciplined life of the pastor. Leaders must work at earning respect in a way that God's people may see *"Christ in you, the hope of glory,"* as found in COLOSSIANS 1:27. A pastor does not start out knowing the people, nor do they know him. And even when they've known a person over time, as in my case as an Associate Minister and Deacon at St. Mark, they don't know how the person will lead when they become the pastor. Pastor Bachus said the pastor earns acceptance by demonstrating his faith in God and by practicing what we preach and teach as we model the life of Christ.

Pastor Bachus shared that leading a congregation comes with many challenges and responsibilities. It's a burden that God places upon a person's shoulders. Pastors are on call 24 hours a day by the flock of God. Our phone is subject to ring at any moment with a member needing prayer, food, financial assistance, housing, or counseling.

One of the things that can lead to burnout in ministry is the amount of time committed to sermon preparation, bible teaching, and bible research. These tasks consume many hours every week, resulting in hours of isolation from family. Social distancing became prevalent with the Coronavirus pandemic, but it is symbolic of how Pastor Bachus spent time away from family and friends due to his devotion and dedication to St. Mark. To avoid burnout, pastors have to exercise wisdom and time management. Finding time to relax and study to hear from the Lord is essential to a pastor's well-being.

Pastors wear a different hat around members than at home. Often the pastor cannot afford to relax too much around members for fear of diminishing his position. Pastor Bachus often attended St. Mark members' birthday and retirement celebrations. However, he would tip out the door before the party got cranked up with loud music and alcohol. I try to follow Pastor Bachus's example and attend gatherings whenever possible. On a few occasions, I've enjoyed a game of Bid Whist!

Pastor Bachus was deeply rooted in his faith and optimistic by nature. He spoke words of life blessings and favor when he counseled members regarding their circumstances. He was known for speaking healing over people and blessings in their lives. He diligently exercised the gift Jesus gave to his apostles, *"And he sent them to preach the kingdom of God, and to heal the sick."* LUKE 9:2 Pastor Bachus' prophetic gift extends to his seed. His granddaughter Tracy Ann Walker often speaks of her visions and dreams regarding God's purposes and plans.

☀

Pastor Bachus believed preaching and teaching take priority over other areas of ministry. "Evangelistic work is highly important in preaching and church growth," he said. Preaching to various religious organizations helps Christians grow in their faith. It was always a blessing to witness him breathe life into a congregation. He was so highly sought after as an evangelist that he preached twenty-one revivals in one year. Pastor Bachus elevated traditional black preaching by blending poetry, parables, and humor with masterful singing and hooping - a rare combination for most preachers. His down-to-earth preaching and approachable personality made it so that everyday people heard him gladly while his reputation spread nationally. "Tell people if you preach," he said, "God will take care of you. God never said I would be James Netters, O. C. Collins, or Kenneth Whalum, but He would take care of me and He's done that much." Pastor Bachus saw himself as a country boy running with the big crowd. "A lot of fine folks always took up with me. I didn't have anything to offer them guys. Pastor Donelson, Pastor Dinkins, and all the big fellows, State Presidents, National Board Members, and Moderators, they gave me honor saying, 'What's going on Bachus!'" I told Pastor Bachus, "You offered them friendship."

  His preaching style was designed to teach about the wages of sin, bring people joy, and exalt the Savior. He believed the primary tool for keeping folks together is preaching and teaching *"What Thus Saith the Lord."* "Preaching is a labor of love for the pastor because he is hearing directly from God to address the needs of the body of Christ," he said.

I readily admit my preaching has evolved and improved over the years. Rev. Dr. Neasbie Alston Sr., one of my many mentors, once told me, "Mims, don't have your sermon so air-tight the Holy Ghost can't slip you something through your side pocket!" He told me this because I relied heavily on my written notes while serving as his Assistant Pastor. More recently, a member of St. Mark told me my preaching style is practical. Traditionally, I connect my sermons with everyday issues and draw analogies to the biblical text. Before becoming pastor of St. Mark, my sermons focused primarily on faith, encouragement, and perseverance. Now I find my sermons focus more on church discipline, respect, humility, unity, love, tithing, and giving. I know firsthand how joyful it is when the Holy Spirit empowers me to speak directly to the congregation in real-time.

When it came to teaching, Pastor Bachus' goal was to let the mind of Christ be in him. He was a walking bible, able to quote scriptures from his head like he was reading from the bible. He repeated scriptures time after time, book, chapter, and verse. He consistently challenged members to learn and memorize one new scripture each week. During weekly bible study, he would start by allowing each member to quote scripture. Sometimes he would allow multiple scriptures from members. Occasionally during Sunday worship, he had members stand and quote their favorite scriptures, he'd expound on them, and that would serve as the message for the day. On Sunday nights during Baptist Training Union (B.T.U.), we played challenging bible games, men competing against women for who could answer the most questions. Racing to be the first to solve quizzes and crossword puzzles was an exciting way to learn for adults and children. Ultimately this prepared us to be armed with the Word of God, just like Jesus was when he faced temptations. *"Let this mind be in you, which was also in Christ Jesus."* PHILIPPIANS 2:5

"There will be times of conflict and envy," he said. "Jesus experienced this with his disciples. When it happens, you must work to avoid it tearing up the peace of your church." I recall seeing Pastor Bachus upset once and an urgent meeting being held with the deacons. I had just been appointed as a deacon and can't remember the exact issue. Whatever it was, it never became a major problem for St. Mark, and it was the only time I ever saw him upset.

The golden rule also applies to being a Shepherd of God's flock, *"And as ye would that men should do to you, do ye also to them likewise."* LUKE 6:31 Pastor Bachus professed people have a desire to be loved and shown respect. "All members are not going to be alike. Some people you have to win over, some people you will never completely win over," Pastor Bachus said, "but the Lord will get you through it.

Jesus did not win the whole crowd. Treat the members right, the best way you can, and go on about your business." He never displayed anger from the pulpit or in public with members. Rarely did church fights happen at St. Mark, or did members hear about them. Pastor Bachus' calm demeanor allowed him to resolve conflict peacefully. If there were disputes or disagreements within the church, he never highlighted them. Consequently, negativity did not have soil to reproduce.

Pastor Bachus also reflected on the importance of pastors being as fair and impartial as possible with members. Pastors get accused of being partial to some members or groups. Nonetheless, Christ spent more time with some of his disciples than others. *"After six days Jesus took Peter, James and John with him and led them up a high mountain, where they were all alone. There he was transfigured before them."* St. Mark 9:2 Pastor Bachus shared, "To be unbiased you have to follow the lead of the Holy Spirit, while also recognizing the individual's unique gifts and faithfulness." We are not biased when relying on those unique gifts is necessary to keep the church moving forward.

Churches experience stress when people can't have their way. Pastor Bachus encouraged pastors to pray for God to lead them in the right direction in every situation. In his view, prayer does not always mean going into your closet or a private space but talking to God where you are. It means having a relationship with Him. For Pastor Bachus, it meant waiting for God to show him how to deal with people based on the scripture so he could help them understand things from a biblical perspective. He said Jesus gave perfect leadership, but no one else can. Even so, there were times Jesus had to be stern in dealing with people. He told the Pharisees, *"Ye are of your father the devil, the lusts of your father ye will do. He was a murderer from the beginning, and abode not in the truth…"* JOHN 8:44 Consequently, there are times the pastor has to address issues publicly and sternly.

I was put in this situation when a member publicly challenged a deacon as he was giving a financial report. This happened twice, catching the deacon off guard both times. I publicly stated the deacon was making a report, not fielding questions. I also informed the congregation that the individual questioning the deacon had direct access to information as a member of the official board. In other words, let's be respectful and fair to those who take on leadership roles to keep St. Mark moving forward. I usually address conflict openly if the situation occurs publicly. If the matter is private, I handle it privately. And I held a church meeting within two months of being appointed pastor. There had not been one for a few years.

Pastor Bachus believed deacons play a significant role in the congregation's spiritual health. Pastors must seek God's guidance in selecting them to avoid a situation where an Official Board's conflict scatters the flock. Maintaining peace and harmony with deacons and other church leaders can be challenging while managing the ambitions of those seeking positions and power in the church. Jesus faced this when the Apostles James and John requested a higher position in the kingdom of God. They petitioned Jesus, *"...Grant unto us that we may sit, one on thy right hand, and the other on thy left hand, in thy glory."* St. Mark 10:35 They were seeking power and influence, things that wouldn't get them into Heaven. Jesus responded by inviting them to serve the people.

Pastor Bachus told me a story about a pastor having a business meeting with the deacons. During the meeting, the pastor said to the deacons, "Brothers, the bible says …" They responded, "We don't want to know what the bible says." Their interests superseded God's plan. Pastor Bachus didn't mince words when he warned that a church struggling with that kind of conflict is headed toward destruction.

Pastor Bachus cautioned against pastors thinking we have to win all battles. "Sometimes you must give in and sometimes you have to stand your ground. You can't always give the flock of God what they want." It is essential to give them what they need and use discernment to see what makes them tick. He referred to the Apostle Paul, who posed a question to the church in ancient Corinth, Greece: *"Why do ye not rather take wrong?"* 1 Cor. 6:7 In other words, instead of haggling over who's right or wrong, sometimes it's better to take the wrong, to accept the injustice so that everyone can move on.

Pastor Bachus reflected on the common causes of church splits. Sometimes people fall out with the preacher and encourage another minister to start a congregation. Sometimes a group in the church can't have their way, so they separate. He believed pastors must do like Jesus and turn the other cheek. Again, pastors can't have their way all the time, and the devil loves tearing up churches. Pastor Bachus understood every church has a personality, some are Pastor-led, some are Deacon-led, and both the Pastor and Deacons lead some. He emphatically believed, "If a man who doesn't know Christ gets in a position of power, he can destroy the church." Jesus told John to write to the angel of the church in Pergamos, *"I know thy works, and where thou dwellest, even where Satan's seat is…"* REV. 2:13. The angel of the church in Pergamos allowed Satan to control his seat, his power, in the church. Pastor Bachus stressed where constant conflict exists, people will leave rather than love and pray for peace.

Another area where churches historically struggle is membership. The loss of members does bother the pastor, but they must minister to the members God sends them and have faith God will sustain them. For various reasons, St. Mark's membership decreased over the last couple of decades. Several St. Mark ministers have either been called to pastor or organized a local assembly. Their family will follow them. Members move out of state, including young adults who attend college elsewhere and decide to remain in that area after graduation or relocate for employment. African Americans in Memphis seem to gravitate to megachurches. We live in an age when people don't value attending church as they did twenty years ago. A global health pandemic was added to the equation in recent years, leaving many people wondering if churches will ever reach their pre-COVID-19 capacity. Amid a pandemic, the church is still summoned to teach, train and evangelize the world for Christ. These challenges aren't limited to St. Mark. Many churches have faced these same issues at some point. However, God has sustained St. Mark during these changing times, blessing us to be debt-free and able to move forward in ministry.

When members depart who tithe or give liberally, the loss of revenue can impact the church's ability to perform ministry. When I talked with Pastor Bachus about the importance of tithing, he gave me strong and honest advice. "None of the members were sold on giving a lot at one time, including me. Been there, done that!" I asked about those who've been on the Deacon Board for several years and don't tithe, including one I mentioned by name. Pastor Bachus reflected on that deacon's many gifts and loyalty and how it would have been wrong to "kick him out the door." The deacon I mentioned started tithing after many years. Pastor Bachus encouraged me to "Keep throwing it in (the subject of tithing). Keep throwing it in! Hit it occasionally in a sermon about the Lord and his goodness. They need to do it, but it must sink in with them. It had to sink in with me!" Pastor Bachus had been preaching for several years before he started tithing.

During Sunday morning worship, he occasionally had tithers stand to encourage non-tithers to tithe. After reflecting on that for a few minutes, he said, "You can mess with some folks and some folks you can't." He went on, "You lay that Word on them. If the Word don't get them, Marvin, it won't last. We are not more powerful than the Word. We were there on some of those bad Sundays with $3 sometimes. But to my knowledge, the church never got behind on a church note."

I experienced something unique and powerful when Pastor Bachus expressed confidence in my leadership and St. Mark's future. "You have the right kind of spirit, in my opinion, to do well with folks," he said. "Everybody will not have a large congregation, Marvin. Don't fall off because somebody doesn't show up. I never thought Bro. (James) Burks would be the man he was, but he turned out to be one of our best men in my opinion. He's just one example. Some of the young guys, they will be alright."

Pastor Bachus proclaimed in all areas of leadership; pastors should pray to God to make the right move. One of his favorite scriptures was, *"In all thy ways acknowledge him, and he shall direct thy paths."* Prov. 3:6. He shared, "God does not quite speak to us like he did Elijah, in a still small voice." Pastor Bachus said that he didn't audibly hear God's voice; God moved on his spirit and heart.

Pastor Bachus admitted the road of the pastor is an incredible journey but sometimes a lonely one. He shared why leaders often experience the Elijah syndrome – feeling alone in what they are trying to accomplish. The reason is that sometimes Satan tries to make pastors think what we do for Christ is in vain. Followers don't appreciate the long hours spent preparing sermons. Friends and relatives don't understand the struggle and the directions we take as pastors. And some people expect much more from a pastor than God put on him. Jesus often went into a solitary place to spend time with his Father. As a leader, a Pastor frequently spends time away from family in prayer and studying to hear from God. He emphasized that during trying times, the Lord promised to be with us if we preach and teach His word; He will provide for our needs: *"...lo, I am with you always, even unto the end of the world."* Matt. 28:20

As Pastor Bachus advised, I find great comfort in knowing God is with me on this journey, and the Lord will always send someone to encourage me and confirm my actions are not in vain.

Although Pastor Bachus announced his retirement in October 2019, it took some time before the transition of leadership was complete. I think in many people's minds, they questioned what my leading the church meant. Pastor Bachus would gradually yield power to me. It was an enormous transition for him, so I allowed him time to adjust. I did not have the traditional celebration of being appointed the new Pastor of St. Mark. It could be the Lord was quickly revealing to me the work to be accomplished and the overwhelming challenges that lay ahead.

After serving for a few months as pastor, Pastor Bachus told me the train had gotten off track. It wasn't a time to celebrate me as the new leader but to help get the train back on track. My life was on an easy street then, and I wasn't sure I was ready for all the work ahead. I had no commitments other than to my wife, grandson Hazen, and German shepherd Kush. Why would I give up the life of living carefree, me and my three? I quickly learned I was not in control of my steps. A scripture states, *"For my thoughts are not your thoughts, neither are your ways my ways, saith the Lord."* ISAIAH 55:8 I can add that God's timing is not always our timing.

My graduate school coursework helped me understand the DNA of St. Mark. When I wrote my graduate paper, *"Why Organizations Refuse to Accept Change, When Change is Necessary for Survival,"* St. Mark was at the forefront of my thoughts. Looking in the rearview mirror, God was preparing me to lead, implement change, and sustain St. Mark during a global pandemic.

Membership shifts eventually happen in many churches with long histories. Generational shifts and changes affected St. Mark's congregation as members grew older. Also, St. Mark hadn't adapted to the changing times. For one, we needed to modify our worship experience. We learned this firsthand from young adults who called a "seat at the table" meeting with church leaders. We needed to hear their concerns. St. Mark still had the traditional 9:30 a.m. to 11:00 a.m. Sunday school. Our 11:00 a.m. worship usually lasted until 1:30 p.m. or 2 p.m. We were no longer the hub for community engagement like in prior years. We didn't offer sports programs that offered a safe place for young people to grow and develop while attracting them to our church.

African-American Baptist churches are known for their traditional church services. To get our train back on track, we needed to reintroduce community engagement in our ministry, recommit ourselves to establishing relationships with the people beyond our walls, and make them feel welcome at St. Mark. We hosted a Pre-Thanksgiving dinner for the community and block parties that we combined with free clothes giveaways. Children were given free school supplies during our Back-to-School Rally. My administration established relationships and partnerships with government officials, nonprofit organizations, business owners, and community leaders to address blight and poverty in South Memphis. We partner with organizations on housing redevelopment plans and ways to provide more resource opportunities to underprivileged individuals. Under my leadership, St. Mark has adopted two Shelby County Schools to provide assistance and resources for children and teachers. I have raised awareness about a specific dilapidated building in South Memphis through numerous media interviews. Now the building is boarded up, and the city keeps the grass cut. St. Mark members contact city officials to have trash in the community removed as part of our commitment to helping South Memphis maintain a safe and clean environment.

      COVID-19 also brought about a lot of change in our church. We held outdoor worship in the church parking lot for two years to help minimize the spread of COVID while allowing members to congregate. We offered free food for people living near St. Mark and numerous COVID-19 vaccination clinics for the community and church members. We began to see more members attending Sunday School and worship when we changed the Sunday school schedule to 50 minutes and reduced our worship time by one hour. These changes allowed for a service filled with spirit and truth that also values our members' time.

When we returned to serving the community, our millennials got excited and rededicated themselves to serving in the church. There is hope! St. Mark is continuing the legacy of Rev. Dr. J. C. Bachus by bridging the church and community as he did during the peak of his leadership.

Pastor Bachus did not panic at the coronavirus, nor was he scared of it. "I honor your right to be cautious," he said. "I am not reckless, but it ain't bothering me." During the height of the pandemic, he preached at the Memphis Baptist Ministerial Association's (MBMA) June 2020 meeting. His sermon was entitled "The Day God Cried." He had just lost one of his dear friends in the ministry, Pastor James Adams, the person who nicknamed him "Cowboy." They were longtime colleagues in ministry and traveling friends. Pastor Bachus' oldest son Patrick questioned his health and strength and tried to get him to back off from preaching at the MBMA meeting. His dad overruled him. "No, son, I've put them off long enough," he said. That same week Pastor Bachus summoned a summer revival at St. Mark and preached with such power and anointing that he easily stood out among the other evangelists. It was as though nobody was going to out-preach him in "The House" the Lord gave him to oversee for over 50 years.

Pastor Bachus had the unique gift to relate any conversation to scriptures in the bible. I shared with him how St. Mark donated $1,000 to MBMA during the pandemic and my vision to keep MBMA a top priority. I mentioned how Rev. J. L. Payne, Dr. Fred Lofton, and Pastor Bachus led the movement to purchase the MBMA building. His response was, "You can't beat Him giving."

The summer of 2020 brought about a change in Pastor Bachus' health. He started getting weaker, to the point where he experienced a serious fall. He spent some time in Methodist Hospital that summer. Seeing how many people were being treated for COVID, he told his doctor at Methodist Hospital, "Y'all doing a good job over here." She was on the COVID Task Force. She thanked him and said, "We're trying." He complimented her on how well she was dressed. She was wearing scrubs and told him she had to change clothes in her garage when she got home to protect her family. He prayed for others when he returned to Methodist Hospital the following month. "My prayers are for all. Prayer changes things," he said. "It changes individuals. It changed me. Prayer is the key to the kingdom; faith unlocks the door."

While visiting Pastor Bachus in the hospital, I called Anita so he could speak to our daughter Tracy. Anita was in Houston visiting Tracy, her husband Joshua, and our grandson Hazen. She was pregnant at that time. Pastor Bachus lit up when he heard Tracy say "Spandaddy," her nickname for him. "Let me talk to Spacey," he said, calling her by the nickname he'd given her as a child. Tracy told him, "Granddaddy, I heard you been making the hospital people laugh!" Pastor Bachus quickly joked, "Yeah, I tell them about Spacey." She chuckled along with him. "You always make me laugh, Granddaddy." Pastor Bachus told her, "You used to sing when you were a little girl… *To Be Like Jesus. It means so much to be like him.*" Tracy said that was her favorite song, and she sang a few notes.

To be like Jesus,

To be like Jesus,

All I ask… To be like Him

All through Life's journey

From Earth to Glory

All I ask … To be like Him.[56]

Pastor Bachus cried quietly on the phone and told her, "I may bring you back to Memphis." She replied with excitement, "You gone bring me back? Bring me back!" She told him she was coming to Memphis in October, and he would have to sing a song with them.

Failing health didn't stop him from being a powerful preacher. I remember his prayer when he visited my brother Don in a nursing

---

56   To Be Like Jesus. Author unknown.

home. Don had rheumatoid arthritis, which had left him unable to walk. "Wait on the Lord! Wait on the Lord," Pastor Bachus prayed. "Be of good strength. He shall strengthen thine heart. Wait I say on the Lord. We don't know what tomorrow holds, but we do know who holds tomorrow!" He encouraged Don to have faith, hope, and trust in the Lord! Miraculously, Don did regain his ability to walk. Pastor Bachus was pleased to see him walk in the door one evening with Anita to visit.

I took Pastor Bachus to numerous medical exams during his last two years. He had a unique gift of making others smile. His wit, humor, and kindness always brought joy to the medical staff. They got a kick from seeing him handsomely dressed, sporting his cowboy hat and cowboy boots. When I jokingly told his Ophthalmologist, Dr. Ana Flores, and her assistant, Ms. Sandra Turner, that they treated him like a king, they both replied, "He is a King!"

Many of my conversations with Pastor Bachus took place at his home with the television show Perry Mason playing in the background, one of Mother Bachus' favorite shows. He loved laughing and joking around with family and teasing Mother Bachus. I asked him one day if Mother Bachus shared the TV remote control with him. He responded, "Now that's the major problem!" According to him, she would come in from the beauty shop and switch away from the show he'd been watching for almost two hours without asking him. Even worse, she waited until the football playoffs to try to understand the game. He said she'd holler at the guy in the black uniform, "Run, run, run!" and then shout the same thing at the guy in the white uniform, "Run, run, run!" According to Pastor Bachus, "She sickin' everybody on everybody saying Get 'em! Get 'em! Get 'em!" Still, if changing the TV channel or ruining a football game was going to start a fight, his advice was, "It's best to just go on somewhere else."

One day he joked with his son Timothy that he knew how to get people off the phone when they wanted to talk and talk. All he had to say was, "Fill out your tithe envelope and send it in!" That would get them off the phone real quick!

Pastor Bachus often expressed concern for all of the members of St. Mark. On occasion, he reminisced or inquired about someone specific. "Some folks believe the Lord, but they don't show much love for Him," he said. "But then there are those like Bro. Sharp." The late Bro. Artis Sharp, a Deacon at St. Mark, was born May 18, 1890. He was 95 years old when he passed on August 21, 1985, and he'd been a member of St. Mark for over 40 years. Pastor Bachus admired and appreciated the deep love that Bro. Sharp had for people. "Bro. Sharp acted in a way he showed love," Pastor Bachus told me. "He loved the church. He loved you." I had the honor and privilege to fall in love with Bro. Sharp as well, and witness his greatness. St. Mark has been blessed with many Saints who lived to be seniors and were faithful for decades.

He asked if Bro. Lee had died. I told him I hadn't seen Bro. Lee since the pandemic. "He used to really get on my nerves," Pastor Bachus said. Bro. Lee was a special needs adult who had some mental challenges. He would ask to speak publicly or pray at the end of worship, putting Pastor Bachus on the spot. Pastor Bachus would often yield and let him say a word or pray. He was loud and would shout and move about uncontrollably during high praise in worship. Pastor Bachus said that when Bro. Lee first started calling him Daddy Bachus, he wanted to tell him, 'I ain't your daddy, boy!' Instead, he learned to love Bro. Lee. He realized he just needed someone to care about him. The congregation admired the kindness and patience he showed Brother Lee and saw it as an example of how we should treat everyone. *"By this shall all men know ye are my disciples if you have love on to another."* ST. JOHN 13:35

Many feared leaving their house during the pandemic. Not Pastor Bachus. We rode by St. Mark one Sunday evening so he could see the church and the new wood fence we had installed on the north side. Anita joined us. He was impressed with how we cleared out trees and improved the landscape at the church. We greeted several members during our visit, who were so glad to see him.

On another short trip, we went to Sonic Drive-In on a Saturday afternoon. Hazen was humming and singing in the back while Pastor

Bachus and I were talking. After a few minutes, Hazen asked me a question. "Papa, why does God love us?" I told him, "I'll let Pastor Great-Great answer that." Pastor Bachus replied, "God loves us because he made us. He made us, Hazen, way back. Way back He made a man." Hazen replied, "A man made of dirt…so alligators and sharks could eat us." Pastor Bachus, never missing a beat, told him, "So little boys could come into the world to grow up to be a man and glorify God, do godly things, think godly, ask godly questions." Hazen continued to hum in the background while we were waiting for our food. Pastor Bachus said to Hazen, "He hears you! He hears you! God hears you now." When the waitress delivered our food, Hazen, filled with joy in receiving his slush, enthusiastically let her know he was Sonic the Hedgehog. She laughed. Hazen said, "Thank you, Papa!" Sonic got his chili dog and fries, I got a chili dog, and Pastor Bachus got ice cream. Hazen blessed the food, we enjoyed it, and we rode back to Pastor Bachus' house.

During a visit with Anita, he told her she has a good husband and to "be good to him." Her response was, "What about me?" Pastor Bachus smiled and told her he would tell me the same thing. He later told me I have a good wife, that she loves me and loves her family. He told me, "Have respect for others, self-respect, a mind to work, and a mind to take care of what God blesses you with. How you treat your children, how you treat your neighbor, is a good example of how you treat God and what He does for you."

As his health began to decline, he made it clear he did not want to burden his family. He talked about it one day in a humorous way. "Children get grown and they have their own families and way of life," he said. "You lived your life, and now you're going to slow theirs down? I don't want every time I need something to say Marvin, Anita, Rodney, Patrick, Timothy… come get me and help me find my house shoes!" All of us were happy to help him find anything he needed. He did not want to pull people away from their daily life and work. When I told him we are called to bear one another's burden, he responded, "So fulfill the love of Christ." He had a knack for finishing scriptures someone else started.

Oct 18, 2020, Hazen prayed for his great-grandfather. "Thank you, God, for Pastor Great-Great. Thank you for Great-Great. Thank you for Papa and Nene and my whole family. In Jesus' name, we pray. Amen." Pastor Bachus replied, "Thank you for that prayer." I requested that he pray for Hazen as well. "Father in heaven, we thank you for this young man. Bless him, and his mother and friends. Bless your people everywhere. Thank you for saving us and giving us a chance to bow before one another, and for healing and touching and deliverance. Bless me in my illness, and my son and grandson, and all the others in their illnesses. We have faith that you will do the things that are right. It may not seem right to us, but if it is right to you, we will accept it, whatever it is. Love us and guide us. In Jesus' name, we pray. Amen."

Pastor Bachus loved singing and preaching and always led family singing around the holidays. During the 2020 Thanksgiving holidays, Hazen and Anita created a song with the words of ST. JOHN 3:16. They sang, *"For God so loved the world, He loved the world, that He gave His only begotten son, that whosoever believeth in Him, believe in Him, should not perish! Not perish! Not Perish! But have everlasting life! Everlasting life! Everlasting life! Everlasting life. Everlasting life! Everlasting life!"* Pastor Bachus joined in singing the scripture they'd set to music until, laughing, he finally said, "Stop! They're killing me!" Hazen laughed with him. His Pastor Great-Great passed down to him the gift of music.

By April 2021, Pastor Bachus was bedridden. He was diagnosed with dementia, but it appeared he had simply reached a place where nothing was left to give. He had given it his all, dedicating most of his 85 years to ministry. His family did their best to make him comfortable. Timothy played some of his favorite songs on an iPad near his bedside. Family members sang along with a recording of *Touch the Hem of His Garment* by Sam Cooke and The Soul Stirrers.

Whoa, there was a woman in the Bible days
She had been sick, sick so very long

> *But she heard 'bout Jesus was passin' by*
>
> *So she joined the gathering throng*
>
> *And while she was pushing her way through*
>
> *Someone asked her, what are you trying to do?*
>
> *She said, if I could just touch the hem of his garment*
>
> *I know I'll be made whole*[57]

On April 4, 2021, Resurrection Sunday, as the family gathered, we listened to Be with Me Jesus, another of Pastor Bachus' favorite songs.

> *Oh Lord, the time is growing nigh*
>
> *When I must breathe my last breath inside*
>
> *Lord, in my dying hour, stay with me, Lord*
>
> *Oh Lord, my friends have gathered 'round*
>
> *They're watching me slowly, slowly sinking down*
>
> *Lord, in my dying hour, stay with me, Lord*[58]

Jesus was with Pastor Bachus as death was approaching, and he was ready to leave his earthly home and enter his home in Heaven to be

---

[57] Cooke, S. (1956). Touch the Hem of His Garment. [Recorded by The Soul Stirrers featuring Sam Cooke]. (45 rpm). Unknown: Specialty Records. 1956. Catalog number SP 896 45

[58] Cooke, S. (1954). Be with Me Jesus. [Recorded by The Soul Stirrers featuring Sam Cooke]. (45 rpm). Unknown: Specialty Records. 1954. Catalog number SP-878.

with the Lord. On April 13, 2021, Rev. Dr. Johnny C. Bachus peacefully departed earth to glory.

On the day of Pastor Bachus' passing, while the family was mourning and meeting, I had to step outside the house to spend an hour on a Zoom meeting at the invitation of John Zeanah, Director of the Memphis and Shelby County Division of Planning and Development. The meeting was held to discuss redevelopment plans for the South City district in Memphis. My goal was to have Rev. J. C. Bachus Boulevard included in those plans. By the grace of God, it was approved. The work of Pastor Bachus was progressing forward even on the day of his death. From building a gym to serve local youth to raising funds for LeMoyne-Owen College, community improvement was one of his hallmark achievements. He was a quiet transformational leader whose impact will be felt for generations.

On Thursday, April 22, 2021, at 5:00 p.m., the Memorial Service for Rev. Dr. Johnny Clarence Bachus was held at St. Mark Missionary Baptist Church where he pastored for 53 years before retiring. The family decided on this service because he touched so many lives with his preaching and teaching, and they wanted his friends and family to have the opportunity to celebrate a life well lived. Dad was a confidant to many people, especially young ministers and Pastors. Hundreds of people from all across the United States came to remember him.

His son, Rev. Rodney C. Bachus Sr., presided over the service. Many reflections, expressions, and tributes were given.

On Friday, April 23, 2021, it was a blessing and honor for me to preside during the Homegoing Celebration for my spiritual leader and champion, Rev. Dr. Johnny Clarence Bachus. The Homegoing Celebration began at 10:00 at St. Mark. It was a glorious praise celebration in honor of a great man of God, who was regarded by many as a type of Moses. His nephew, Rev. Alvin Casey, was sergeant-at-arms. National and local pastors offered expressions and reflections. His brother, Rev. Clemmie L. Bachus of Kansas City, Kansas, was the eulogist. Pastor Bachus' 12 grandchildren (aka the 12 Disciples) rendered a special tribute in his honor. His granddaughters sang an amazing rendition of *Closer to Jesus*, a song written by their granddaddy and the title song on the album St. Mark's Mass Choir released in 1980. Bro. Lee, who I hadn't seen since the start of the pandemic, was among the mass of people who came to celebrate Pastor Bachus' life and homegoing. The repass was also at St. Mark, with many family members, friends, and church members in attendance.

Left to cherish his memory are his beautiful wife of sixty-three years, Mrs. John Ella Bachus; two daughters, Johnnie Ruth Griggs and Anita (Marvin) Mims Sr.; three sons, Patrick (Shep) Bachus, Rodney (LaTanya) Bachus Sr., and Timothy Bachus; twelve grandchildren, eighteen great-grandchildren; one sister, Lucille (Al) Smith; two brothers, Rev. Clemmie L. Bachus and Herman (Carolyn) Bachus; sister-in-law, Marie Bachus; sister-in-law, brother-in-law, Johnny (Tina) Johnson, Jr; and a host of relatives and friends.

He kept the faith and finished his course. He is with Jesus now.

TRIBUTES TO
REV. DR. JOHNNY CLARENCE ("J.C.") BACHUS

Deacon Patrick Bachus, Eldest Son

Thank you, Brother! I appreciate you putting our father's life into a written "Legacy." I would like to thank my father for being a champion in my life. He was a great gift to me, both at home and church. He was a physical and spiritual gift. My life today is better because he was in my life. He made me "some count"!

Rev. Rodney Clarence Bachus Sr., Son

I remember one time I had a chance to sing with this R & B group that was going on tour, traveling to 4 or 5 cities! My children were young and needed their father, so I asked Daddy should I take the chance going on the road and leaving my family to support them. He told me he had the same opportunity that Elvis Presley had and he asked his mother what to do. She told him, "Johnny, God will provide." And that's what he shared with me! "Rodney, God will provide."

Timothy Bachus, Son

My college provost, college Chaplain and young preachers at Philander Smith College asked about him constantly. He spoke at my high school commencement the year prior to my graduating. The speech was entitled, "Mr. Big Stuff, who do you think you are?" One of my friends talked about it for years. Dad was a fierce, powerful preacher that never took himself too seriously. He was a good brother, uncle, and true patriarch in our family. All that I have done, overcome, and achieved; I see his impact on everything. They loved me through all my college faults and failures, they loved me through it all! I'll never forget that!

Rev. Alvin L. Casey, Nephew, Charlotte, NC

Pastor Bachus was the hardest preaching preacher that I knew. Anytime he had preached somewhere, even if I didn't know for sure he had preached, I could still tell that he had because there was an aura around him. He was on a different plane or a different level and that always impressed me. I always depended on my ear to hear God when I preached, because I always wanted to be in the spirit like that, and I received that from Pastor Bachus. The opportunity to grow up with him and know him was special. Associate Minister, St. Mark Baptist Church.

Sis. Mamie Richmond, Longtime Member, St. Mark Baptist Church, Memphis, TN

Reverend Bachus' humble beginnings can be traced back to his birth in Hernando, MS, and his acceptance of Christ at the age of eleven. As Pastor, he was a sainted servant and a dynamic pastor with a yearning for spiritual growth. His love and dedication are not forgotten; they are still being felt at Saint Mark as well as other areas where he traveled throughout the United States. Reverend Bachus was a friend to everyone and always displayed God's love. His leadership through Christian education has led to many souls being saved and inspired.

Rev. Dr. Frank E. Ray Sr., Senior Pastor, New Salem Baptist Church, Memphis, TN

It was at my home church, Hammond Grove in Arlington, TN, at the age of twenty, when I met a quiet and gentle spirit man by the name of Dr. Johnny Clarence Bachus. I discovered an intellectual person when he spoke, and I was blown away by his singing capability. As time progressed, we became friends when he conducted revivals in the areas.

In my early ministry, he became the President of the Baptist Ministerial Association of Memphis, TN, where I quickly rushed to be under his leadership. He then became Moderator of the Memphis District Association, and I joined it as well.

Dr. Bachus was one of those persons that, to me, was a mentor, a role model, a motivator, and a mirror. I saw him walk into many hostile meetings and with his charismatic spirit and humble attitude, he was able to quiet the storms. I witnessed him taking a small St. Mark Church and transforming it into a major ministry. He was a preacher-leader who engaged himself in social justice, soul-winning, and men-building.

Finally, after I became a pastor and whatever I went through when the wolves were howling, and the dogs were barking, I knew I had a friend that would always have an encouraging word for me, and his name was Dr. Johnny Clarence Bachus, whom I will forever love and cherish.

Rev. Dr. Edward Parker Jr., Pastor Emeritus, Berean Missionary Baptist Church, Memphis, TN

The Man and His Legacy. Our families are from the same area of Mississippi. His brother Rev. Dr. C. L. Bachus worked with my dad at one time in Memphis. When I originally formed Berean Baptist Church, I immediately wanted to join the Memphis District Association led by Pastor Bachus. I became a member of the Association due to his personality and his love and care for people. He was good at mentoring and family traditions. I felt at home in his company. When I went through a church split, he stayed my friend and our churches would fellowship together when some distanced themselves from me. Pastor Bachus worked at letting folks be themselves. He was his own person. Pastor Bachus gave great leadership to the Believers of Jesus Christ and forevermore his imprint on Christian Ministry will have an everlasting memory on those he left behind, not only here in Memphis, Tennessee, but to those all across the United States of America.

Rev. Dr. Randolph Meade Walker, Senior Pastor, Castalia Baptist Church, Memphis TN

Johnny Clarence (J. C.) Bachus was a very gifted pastor. He came from the classic mold of so many African American Mississippi-born preachers who blessed America. So many preachers from the South, like his brother Clemmie, went North or West in the Great Black Migration. However, J. C. stayed true to his native South where he served as pastor of the St. Mark Baptist Church of Memphis, Tennessee, for fifty-three years.

He was a fiery evangelical preacher who was constantly in demand as a revivalist. He also had the phenomenal gift of singing. These double endowments of ability caused him to be a favorite among church goers who loved traditional gospel music and preaching. He was known for being able to sing songs that had not been heard in years, but were still cherished.

Outside of the pulpit, Bachus was a favorite of fellow clergy and the laity. He had a winsome sense of humor. As a spellbinding storyteller, he could entertain an informal audience for an extended period with joyful anecdotes taken from the Black Church experience.

Bachus was a faithful supporter of all levels of his denominational affiliations. He was a regular participant of the Memphis District Association, Tennessee Baptist Missionary and Educational Convention, and the National Baptist Convention, U.S.A., Inc. He had the historic distinction of being the third president of the Memphis Baptist Ministerial Association.

He was a friend to many people. He was known for keeping up with aging and ailing preachers. He was so accommodating and amicable that his friendship was valued across the country.

Rev. Dr. Ricky Dugger Sr., Pastor, Norris Avenue Missionary Baptist Church, Memphis, TN, President of the Memphis Baptist Ministerial Association:

I am grateful for knowing Pastor J C Bachus – the Pastor of the St. Mark Baptist Church, and former President of the Memphis Baptist Ministerial Association. He was an ideal leader for the preacher of today. His wisdom and leadership exemplified great resilience, and he was an example for me and others to follow. His profound statement to me once: "You use what you have for the glorification of God. It will work out for your good." He was a good man of conversation, very much celebratory in his conduct and character.

Rev. Dr. Vernon L. Horner, Pastor, Greater New Bethel Baptist Church, Memphis, TN, Former President of the Memphis Baptist Ministerial Association

Dr. J. C. Bachus was one of the greatest preachers I ever had the privilege of sharing the pulpit with. He was always encouraging and very supportive. He was an excellent role model for those of us who were coming along behind him. I felt it was a privilege to share the same pulpit with him. On one occasion I told him, "Dr. Bachus I feel like I ought to be sitting and listening and you preaching," and he told me, "No, Bro. President, it's your hour to preach." And I felt very blessed just to be on the same program with one of God's greatest preachers. Pastor Rev. Dr. J. C. Bachus, may God bless the legacy and memory of this great man of God. Earth's loss was heaven's gain.

Rev. James Van Buren, Pastor, Mt. Carmel Missionary Baptist Church, Memphis, TN

I have pastored one church for thirty-nine years. At the beginning of my pastorship, I met Pastor J. C. Bachus. He was one of the great influences on my success as a pastor. Pastor Bachus immediately shared with me that I would encounter some victories and some defeats. He said I was to remain faithful to the assignment despite the outcome. Pastor Bachus also shared the importance of being yourself in all situations, such as teaching, preaching, etc. He was a great asset to me.

Pastor Ronald Hampton, Right Direction Christian Ministries, Memphis TN

If there was ever a model for a Gospel preacher, Pastor J. C. Bachus would certainly fit the mold. Probably and arguably one of the Godfathers of Pastor/Preachers in Memphis in an era when pastors were held in high esteem. While Pastor Bachus held several positions during his years as pastor of the St. Mark Baptist Church, I saw a man who was ever humble and regarded the pulpit as a sacred place, and he determined to grace it every Sunday morning.

I once asked him what advice he could give me as a young pastor and his reply was to just love the people. I think in many ways what he was telling me is to find and be myself as a pastor, but relationships were what I would need to build the membership. The Gospel message would take care of itself. This tall gentle man as I knew him could take a common scenario and build a life-changing message with it. And as a vocalist, Pastor Bachus could sing the church into a hallelujah shout.

Pastor Bachus will be missed for years to come by family, friends, and acquaintances. However, his face will always be on the walls of the St. Mark Church to remind all who enter the edifice to forever feel his presence.

Pastor Jairus Prince Winfrey Sr., Greater Mt. Zion Missionary Baptist, Memphis TN

My first ministerial contact with Pastor J. C. Bachus occurred on Monday, March 4, 2013, at Shiloh Church of Memphis during a City Union #2 meeting. It was twenty-two days after I had preached my first sermon. Nervously filling in for my pastor, I preached a sermon entitled "Yes We Can." After the message, Dean Bachus encouraged me, inspired me and loved on me. He also led the perfect song to incapsulate the sermon. On March 2, 2020, again at Shiloh Church, the Lord solidified my relationship with Pastor Marvin Mims, my beloved Brother/Friend/Fishing Buddy/Sparing Partner. Now my mission with Pastor Bachus' family, namely Hazen, is to encourage them, inspire them and love them like Pastor Bachus did me.

ACKNOWLEDGMENTS

Thanks be unto God for the completion of this book. This work was accomplished with the help of many family members. I want to start by thanking my awesome wife. Anita's supportive companionship has been loving and faithful for decades. She is the superglue that keeps the family bonded with her prayers and inspirational Sunday morning text messages. Thanks for birthing four blessed children into this world and being a dynamic grandmother. People often tell you, "You are good for putting up with Marvin!" Now I can put it in print! Thanks for your prophetic voice in my life. You inspired me to write, proofread all of my material and helped to research your dad's life. Thank you for recalling our life journey. Thank you so much, Black Boo!" Love, Marvin

    I am enormously indebted to Mrs. John Ella Bachus, my mother-in-law, for providing facts and details about Pastor Bachus' life and ministry. Your representation as the First Lady of St. Mark has been a shining example for pastors' wives throughout the City of Memphis. Your love, teaching, faith, example, and determination are a blessing to our family.

    I am extremely appreciative of our remarkable children, Takenya

Anica Mims, Marvin Bachus Mims Jr., Joshua Desmond Walker, and Tracy Ann Walker. You are deeply loved by your mom and me. Thanks for your assistance in this project and lighting up our lives with (Dad subsidized) dinners, parties, and family celebrations. You are incredible children and our treasure. Joshua, thanks for the initial draft design of my book cover.

A special thanks to our baby girl, Tracy Ann Walker, "Persuader in Chief," for your excellent editing. Thanks for painstakingly challenging me to dig deep in my writing and be specific in citing details. Thanks for pulling facts and elements out of my brain, sending me into four years of research, and organizing my material into a good working draft. You should have been a lawyer! Thanks for constantly reminding me profoundly when I wanted to get done, "You can't rush greatness!" God has gifted and anointed you with many talents as a leader!

I want to thank my uncle Robert Russell Sr., my cousin Sandy Clifton Russell Jr., and my siblings, Angela Mims and Morris Mims, for providing valuable, historical information about our Russell and Mims family. My siblings' memories, recollections of our family history, and facts helped me include key pieces in my book. Thanks for your support of my ministry spiritually and financially. Thanks for the family love!

I am thankful to LaJoyce Harris for her editorial work, guiding me down a path of structure and organization in my writing composition, and enhancing my sermons for three years during the pandemic so I could reach saints virtually. Thank you for the constructive comments that improved my thinking and writing and for helping me expand and market my ministry!

I am thankful to Charlotte Juantina Bachus for your assistance with this book and for serving as a personal assistant. Your technological expertise and promotion of my book and ministry are a blessing. Thanks for proofreading my prerecorded conversations with your uncle, Pastor Bachus.

I am thankful for our church secretary, VaShelia (Shep) Bachus, and my administrative assistant, Sydrea Bryson, who helped manage the day-to-day operations at St. Mark while I pursued this work!

I am appreciative of Lebanon Raingam (Nonon Tech & Design) for his assistance in formatting my book for publishing.

I appreciate my brothers-in-law, Rev. Rodney C. Bachus Sr., Deacon Patrick Bachus, and Timothy (Karaoke King) Bachus, for their close relationship for many years and the opportunity to share in the rich family legacy with the Bachus family.

Hazen and Addison (Happy)! You both bring great joy to your grandparents' lives. Your praise, prayers, caring spirits, smile, and humor light up a room. Your imaginations, talents, and creativity will take you farther than you can dream. This legacy of your granddad, great-granddads, great-great-grandfathers, and great-great-great grandfathers, gives you a road map to follow, with God's favor on your life. You have inherited unique gifts from your ancestors. Walk in your anointing!

I am grateful to the St. Mark Baptist Church family for my spiritual growth, nurture, education, and empowerment as a deacon, associate minister, and pastor. I am thankful for the church of my spiritual birth, New Mount Zion Missionary Baptist Church, and the late Rev. H. A. Armstrong in Greenville, MS, for my childhood biblical learning and development. I am thankful to the Greater Mount Olive Missionary Baptist Church in Lebanon, IL, and their Pastor, Rev. Dr. W. J. Griffin, for the love they gave a young married couple while we were away from family in the early 80s. I am grateful to Gospel Temple Missionary Baptist Church, the late Rev. Dr. Neasbie Alston, and his wife, the late Dr. Bettye Alston, for entrusting me to assist Pastor Alston. I am grateful to my new pastor, Rev. Dr. David Ricks, and the Robinhood Lane Baptist Church for accepting me as a member.

I am thankful for the following contributors: Rev. Dr. David Ricks, Rev. Dr. Rickey L. Dugger, Sr., Elder Archie L. Thomas, Rev. Dr. Frank E. Ray, Rev. Dr. Melvin Charles Smith, Rev. Dr. Edward Parker Jr., Rev. Dr. Randolph Meade Walker, Rev. Dr. Vernon. L. Horner, Pastor

James Van Buren, Rev. Alvin L. Casey, Pastor Ronald Hampton, Pastor Jairus Prince Winfrey Sr., Bro. Herman Bachus, Sis. Anita Mims, Mrs. John Ella Bachus, Sis. Mamie Richmond, and Deacon Preston Pittman.

During the COVID-19 pandemic, my life has been enriched by family and friends, along with the pastors and preachers with the Memphis Baptist Ministerial Association and the members of City Union # 2, from whom I gain spiritual insight and inspiration weekly. I thank all of you!

A special thanks to my final editor, Lynn Ballard. Lynn has a BA in Mass Media Communication from the University of Akron and a Master's in Public Administration from Auburn University, where she taught American Government as a Presidential Fellow. As a parachute contributor and professional wordsmith, she applies broad knowledge, experience, and creativity to projects across the disciplines, from co-writing two televised documentaries about young jazz musicians to editing the feasibility study submitted to Congress for the Tuskegee Airmen National Historic Site. Thank you, Lynn, for accepting this assignment at the eleventh hour, transforming this book, and becoming family along the way. Autobiography is hard because it pulls back the layers of your life. Thank you, my sister, for helping me do that with grace and humor, and always landing me safely.

Lastly, it was an honor to document the life of the late Rev. Dr.

Johnny C. Bachus, one of the greatest humanitarians this world has ever known, and the connections in our lives. I am thankful Pastor Bachus gave me a view into his life as a man, husband, father, grandfather, great-grandfather, pastor, preacher, prophet, priest, mentor, and friend before his departure to glory!

ims Ordination as a Deacon at
Mark Church by Pastor Bachus

Pastor Bachus and Mrs. Bachus

Astros Game

Mims at
Mandela Monument,
Johannesburg,
South Africa

Mims and Russell Cousins
Riverside, California

Kent Russell at St Mark
Baptist Church

Pastor Bachus Preaching
the Gospel of Christ

Mims and Anita in
Johannesburg,
South Africa

Pastor Winfrey, Hazen and Mims Fishing

at St. Mark

Mims, Pastor W.J
Griffin,
Greater Mt. Olive

Grandmother, Mrs. Love

hus

la Bachus

Hazen and Addison

Mims, Sandy
Clifton
Russell, 2022

Mims and
Anita
Graduating
together

Mims
Family,
Houston,
Tx

Addison's Baby Dedication,
October 2020

Mims
Family,
Early Years

cing, Anita in South Africa

Pastor Bachus with Hazen

Mims & Anita Capetown, South Africa 2019

Mims and Russell Family October 2021

Hazen's Confession of faith at St. Mark Baptist Church

Mrs. Mims and Johnella

Mims & Mom

Mims with Mrs. Brother and

Dating, Mims & Anita in 1980

Pastor BACHUS and Mims conducting Baptismal

Marvin Mims Sr. & Marvin Mims Jr.

Pastor Thomas and First Lady with Children

Granddaddy Russell

Mims Family, Oct 2019

Mims with Pastors Hampton Thomas and Crutcher

Road to Granddaddy Russell house

Mims and Anita Malibu, Califonia

Tereather Addie Mims (Mom) And Marvin Mims Jr. Family Reunion Phoenix, Arheic

Mims Parents, Anita and Marvin Sr.

Certificate of License

Preacher's Licience

Hazen's Baptism

Hazen and Papa in Chattanooga 2019

Mrs. Tereather Addi Mims, Mother, Pastor Bachus in background

Mims at Mt. Baldy, California

CPSIA information can be obtained
at www.ICGtesting.com
Printed in the USA
LVHW010031251022
731458LV00003B/4